GONCHAROVA

GONCHAROVA
Stage Designs and Paintings

Mary Chamot

Oresko Books Limited

(frontispiece)
Self-portrait with Yellow Lilies
MOSCOW, Tretyakov Gallery. 1907. Oil on canvas 77 × 58·2 cm.

The artist is seen against a wall covered with paintings. Like most young artists she often painted herself for lack of other models. The eager expression, which remained with her to the end of her days (fig. 12), is vividly rendered and may reflect the first triumph of success. This portrait is one of several works she gave to the Tretyakov Gallery in 1927 when some of her paintings, left in Russia, were sent out to her.

ACKNOWLEDGEMENTS

I would like to express my gratitude to all those who have helped me in preparing this book and who gave me photographs and permission to reproduce works in their possession, beginning with the artist herself, whom I had the privilege of visiting on many occasions during the last years of her life, and with Richard Buckle, who lent me a number of rare photographs of works which had figured in the Diaghilev Exhibition organized by him in 1954–55. Without the generous assistance of Madame Alexandra Larionov the task would have been impossible. Dr. John Bowlt kindly lent me the records of exhibitions he compiled during his studies in Moscow and put me in touch with other art historians, especially Dr. D. V. Sarabianov. Mr. Eugene Mollo gave me an account of his meetings with Larionov and lent me a number of his letters. Mrs. Evelyn Antal kindly read the original text and made many useful suggestions. Finally, I would like to thank the staff of the following collections for facilitating my studies: the Victoria and Albert Museum; the Tate Gallery; the Theatre Museum and the archives of Covent Garden, Messrs Sotheby Parke Bernet & Co. and the Piccadilly Gallery, London; the Tretyakov Gallery and the Bakhrushin Central Theatre Museum, Moscow; the Russian Museum, Leningrad; the Musée d'Art Moderne, Centre Pompidou, Paris; and Mademoiselle Evelyne Cournand, Paris; the Museum of Modern Art and the Solomon R. Guggenheim Museum, New York and the librarians of the Slavonic Departments in the Universities of London and Cambridge. I am most grateful to Robert Oresko for his editorial care and enthusiasm. Despite all my efforts and those of the publisher, it has proved impossible to trace the present whereabouts of every picture reproduced in this book, and the publisher and I would like to apologize to the current owners for our lack of success.

Sincere thanks are also due to the following for their help in providing photographs and information: A. J. Richards, London; British Library, London; Dan Flavin, Garrison, New York; Grosvenor Gallery, London; L. B. Tobin, San Antonio, Texas; Leonard Hutton Galleries, New York; Kazan Museum, Kazan; Musée des Beaux-Arts, Ville de Lyon; Museum of Fine Arts, Richmond, Virginia; Museum of Modern Art, New York; National Art Library, Wellington, New Zealand; National Library, Vienna; National Museum of Wales, Cardiff; Omsk Art Gallery, Omsk; Staatsgalerie, Stuttgart; Scottish National Gallery of Modern Art, Edinburgh; Solomon R. Guggenheim Museum, New York; Sotheby Parke Bernet & Co., London; Tate Gallery, London; Temple Gallery, London; Victoria & Albert Museum, London; Wadsworth Atheneum, Hartford.

First published in Great Britain in 1979 by
ORESKO BOOKS LIMITED
167 Hermitage Road, London N4 1LZ.

ISBN 0 905368 52 5

Abbreviations

As it has not been possible to illustrate all the works mentioned, reproductions in other publications are referred to in abbreviated form, giving author, date and page, plate or catalogue number. The abbreviations are:

A.C.:	Arts Council exhibition catalogue *Larionov and Goncharova.* Leeds, Bristol, London, 1961.
C.G.:	Camilla Gray, *The Great Experiment 1863–1922.* London, 1971.
M.C.:	Mary Chamot, *Gontcharova.* Paris, 1972.
T.L.:	Tatiana Loguine, *Gontcharova et Larionov.* Paris, 1971.
Hutton, 1968:	Leonard Hutton Galleries exhibition catalogue *Fauves and Expressionists.* New York, 1968.
Hutton, 1971:	Leonard Hutton Galleries exhibition catalogue *Russian Avant-garde 1908–1922.* New York, 1971.

GONCHAROVA

NATALIA GONCHAROVA WAS fortunate in beginning her career in Moscow at a time when exceptional interest was shown in the arts. In the late nineteenth century the old Russian capital had produced a new class of patrons, not rulers or aristocrats as before, but wealthy merchants and industrialists. Often descended from peasant stock, with an innate taste for splendour, but without upper-class conventions, they were not afraid to launch out in startling directions in their collecting zeal. Instead of concentrating on Old Masters, they turned to exciting aspects of contemporary art and to old icons, which had scarcely been considered as works of art before. The 'Old Believers' religious sect were among the first to collect icons for their artistic merit and in 1913 an extensive exhibition of icons was held in Moscow, as part of the Romanov tercentenary exhibition celebrations. This exhibition was a revelation to Goncharova and to other artists of her generation.

The first of the new patrons was Pavel Tretyakov (1832–1898) who built up a collection of Russian paintings and gave it to the city of Moscow. Though now owned by the State, it still bears his name and reflects his taste for the didactic, realistic and sometimes anecdotal work of the *Peredvizhniki,* a group of painters known in the West as 'Wanderers', 'Travellers' or 'Ambulants'. In order to reach a wider public, they organized exhibitions of their works in provincial cities, as well as in Moscow and St. Petersburg. Some of them were strongly Slavophile. Their narrative pictures often exposed the abuses under the old régime, such as drunken priests and dying convicts, and they tended to pay little attention to formal and decorative qualities.

Another member of a wealthy Moscow family, Alexei Bakhrushin, developed a very personal interest in the theatre. His forebears had amassed a fortune by supplying army boots during the Turkish wars. The remarkable collection he formed is still preserved in his house as the nucleus of the Bakhrushin Central Theatre Museum, which now also contains a number of works by Goncharova.

The art of the theatre was also given valuable encouragement by the railway magnate Savva Mamontov (1841–1918). He turned his estate at Abramtsevo into a centre of artistic activity, which flourished until the end of the century. Painters, sculptors and musicians were invited to spend the summer months at his house. In the evenings the company used to read books and plays aloud, which led to private theatricals and finally to the creation of Mamontov's private opera in Moscow. It opened in January 1885 with a production of the *Mermaid* [*Rusalka*] by Dargomyzhsky, with scenery and costumes by Viktor Vasnetsov. The unity of artistic effect and quality of dramatic action and singing were far better than in the Imperial theatres. The success of Rimsky-Korsakov's opera *Sadko* stimulated him to write *The Tsar's Bride* and *Tsar Saltan* for Mamontov. It was at the private opera that Chaliapine made his name and Mussorgsky, whose music had been disparaged, became popular. Another of Mamontov's protégés was that strange genius Mikhail Vrubel (1856–1910) who first met his future wife, the opera singer Zabela, at Abramtsevo and was much admired by Goncharova and all the younger generation of artists for his imagination, jewel-like colours and almost Cubist construction of form, long before the Cubist movement began (figs. 1 and 2).

By far the most spectacular collectors in Russia during the first decade of the twentieth century were the two Moscow textile manufacturers, Morozov and Shchukin. Ivan Morozov (1871–1921) began by buying Russian pictures, he owned Goncharova's *Boys Skating* (Plate 11), and gradually turned his attention to the French Impressionists, Post-Impressionists, Nabis and Fauves. He acquired no less than eighteen works by Cézanne and commissioned Maurice Denis and Bonnard to decorate his house in Moscow. His older but more adventurous friend, Sergei Shchukin (1854–1937), was one of five brothers, all of whom collected pictures, but he alone had the perspicacity to buy the most avant-garde modern works. Both Morozov and Shchukin frequently visited Paris, until the 1914–18 war put a stop to their collecting. In 1911 when Matisse came to stay with Shchukin in Moscow, he was full of admiration for the icons he saw and declared that French artists should come to Russia to study, rather than go to Italy. It was of vital importance for Russian art that young artists and students were allowed to see these collections, as well as all the exhibitions held in Moscow during that decade. On Sundays Shchukin himself used to hold forth about his pictures, explaining the latest developments in Paris. Not surprisingly the effect of these visits undermined the very foundations of academic teaching, aroused violent discussions, excited youth and produced an immediate flow of imitations. The situation in Moscow must have been comparable to that which occurred in Western Europe when, after the 1939–45 war, the first examples of modern American abstract art were exhibited. Against this background Larionov and Goncharova began their careers.

Natalia Goncharova was a child of the Russian countryside. She was born in Negaevo in 1881 and spent much of her childhood at Ladyzhino, her grandmother's estate in the province of Tula, in the very centre of Russia. Her father, Sergei Goncharov, was an architect and the family was descended from Afanasy Goncharov, who in the reign of Peter the Great had invented a loom large enough to make sails for the new Russian navy and founded the first linen factory in Russia. A town called Polotnyany [linen] has grown up on the site where the Goncharov family had their estate and factories. The large three-storied eighteenth-century house had accommodated Catherine the Great in 1775 and later the poet Pushkin stayed there after his marriage to an earlier Natalia Goncharova. The family fortune had been dissipated in the 1790s by a spendthrift, who, among other extravagances, had maintained a private orchestra. Natalia Goncharova was to spend some of her happiest and most productive summers at Polotnyany Zavod, the family home. Her mother, Yekaterina Belyaeva, came from a family of priests and Natalia prided herself on the tradition of a gipsy strain on this side of her family, which may account for a mystical trait in her character, a tendency to superstition and a love of remote antiquity. As a child she was deeply affected by the variety of customs still current among the Russian peasantry at that time. The colourful clothes they wore, their singing and dancing, the delightful toys and wooden utensils they made during the winter months, the solemn ceremonial in the village church and its icons left indelible impressions, later reflected in her art. A vast store of folklore, drawn from ancient legends or brought from the East by traders or Mongol invaders, was still kept alive by word of mouth among the people. She loved the stories related to her and her younger brother by their nurse and by Dmitry the *dvornik* [outdoor handyman], who as a soldier had seen service in many parts of Russia. He delighted the children with an inexhaustible fund of songs and stories. Some of these stories had been set down in poetic form by Pushkin and were to be illustrated by Goncharova in theatrical productions and in books. Through the family link with the poet, it is not surprising that for Natalia, more than for most Russian children, Pushkin became the best known and most loved poet.

The thrill when the first blades of grass appeared between patches of melting snow and the sudden blossoming forth of nature, after the long months of winter, never failed to fill her with joy. Half a century spent in cities had not dimmed the memory of the country she loved. Even in her old age, her face lit up when she recalled the delight she had felt in her youth at the coming of spring.

It was a wrench to be taken from this happy environment and sent to school in Moscow at the early age of eleven. During this period she lived in the family town house at 8 Trekhprudny Lane, next door to the poet Marina Tsvetaeva (1892–1941). Although they attended the same school, they hardly knew each other at the time as Marina was ten years younger, but in 1928 they met in Paris and Tsvetaeva has recorded a

fig. 1 Mikhail VRUBEL
Portrait of Savva Mamontov
Moscow, Tretyakov Gallery. 1897. Oil on canvas 187 × 142·5 cm.

Vrubel's vigorous and highly imaginative work was a great inspiration to young artists in the early twentieth century. They saw the germ of Cubism in his blocking out of forms. Mamontov's patronage extended to artists and musicians, and his private opera in Moscow did much to raise the standard of productions in Russia.

fig. 2 Mikhail VRUBEL
Swan Princess
Moscow, Tretyakov Gallery. 1900. Oil on canvas 142·5 × 93·5 cm. Signed bottom right in Russian: Vrubel 1900.

Vrubel had designed sets and costumes for Rimsky-Korsakov's opera *Tsar Saltan* for Mamontov and this image of the Swan Princess is one of his most evocative creations. The features of his wife Zabela appear under the glittering jewelled headgear as the white wings seem to float over the dark sea.

detailed, though somewhat poetic, account of Goncharova's life and art (*Prometei*, Moscow, 1969, pp. 144–201). Much of the information in the present work is derived from this memoir. An autobiography by Goncharova herself was deposited in the Tretyakov Gallery after her death, but was not available for consultation.

On finishing school Natalia decided to continue her studies. Higher education for women was a comparative novelty in Russia at the time. She attended some courses on history, zoology and botany, thought of following her father's profession, and finally did the next best thing by entering the department of sculpture in the Moscow School of Painting, Sculpture and Architecture. There she had the good fortune to study under Prince Pavel Troubetskoi, the most original sculptor then working in Russia. He had spent much of his life abroad, was influenced by Rodin and Medardo Rosso and revolutionized the teaching of art by encouraging his students to study nature rather than casts and objects in museums.

Ever since childhood Goncharova had been fond of drawing and she had a few lessons in painting from a pupil of the landscape painter Levitan. Yet she firmly asserted that she had arrived at an understanding of painting by herself and had only studied sculpture at the art school. She claimed that it was the French painters who opened her eyes to the great traditions of her own country. After three years of study, interrupted by ill health, she won a silver medal for sculpture and left the school, although the prescribed period of study at that time was ten years.

Of far greater importance for her future career than her achievements in sculpture was her meeting with Mikhail Larionov. He had entered the art school the same year as she had, but in the painting faculty, and was to be her lifelong companion and partner in many epoch-making undertakings. They certainly knew each other by 1900, when, according to Eganbury who wrote the first monograph on both artists, Larionov painted four portraits of her. Together they drew animals at the zoo and discovered the stimulus of modern French painting and of early Russian art, icons as well as folk art. It was under Larionov's guidance and with his encouragement that she began to paint, first in pastel, later in oil and watercolour.

In 1903 she accompanied Larionov to his home in Tiraspol in the Ukraine and they sailed round the Crimea. The first sight of the South was a revelation to her. She had never seen the sea before. She was struck by its colour and movement, resembling that of grass blown by the wind in the fields. The rich vegetation and the colourful inhabitants, especially the Tartars and Jews in their oriental costumes, were equally exciting. In 1916, when she visited Spain, the Spanish Jews reminded her of the ones she had seen in southern Russia. No paintings of this journey appear to have survived and perhaps none were produced.

The extent and variety of her early work can be judged only from the list given by Eganbury in his monograph on Goncharova and Larionov. This list corresponds very closely with the catalogue of Goncharova's first one-woman exhibition of 1913 and can be regarded as fairly reliable. The artist herself must have supplied it, as well as the note on her artistic development, which reads: '1901–1906 period of Impressionism and Divisionism; 1906–1911 period of Synthesis, Cubism and Primitivism; from 1911 Futurism and Rayonism'. In 1902, while still working as a sculptor, Goncharova began to paint. Several portraits and landscapes are listed. In 1937 in an interview with Jean Maréchal (*Le Petit Parisien*, 23 June 1937) she said that she gave up sculpture because it was an art in which the means of expression were too limited: 'Sculpture cannot convey the emotion produced by a landscape, the moving fragility of flowers, the softness of a sky in spring. I renounced it also because I was fascinated by the play of light, the harmonies of colour.'

Some of the earliest works by Goncharova reflected the delicate nostalgia of a group of artists who, in 1907, held a single exhibition under the title *The Blue Rose* [*Golubaya Rosa*]. The movement derived from the neo-romantic Moscow painter, Viktor Borisov-Musatov (1870–1905) and enjoyed the patronage of the wealthy and sybaritic industrialist Nikolai Ryabushinsky, himself an amateur painter. He financed the magnificent art journal *Golden Fleece* [*Zolotoye Runo*], published from 1906 to 1909, and a series of exhibitions under the same name. Goncharova did not exhibit with *The Blue Rose*, but was evidently attracted by their love of symbolism and their taste for the fashions of the past (Plate 1). During these years she also painted straightforward naturalistic studies of still-life and flowers, which found ready sales among collectors, artists and writers. Owners of her early work, listed by Eganbury, include two members of the well-known Morozov family, the artists Kandinsky and Milioti and the leader of Symbolism in Russian literature, Valery Bryusov. Some of the works recorded under various owners may have been presented as gifts or by way of exchange. It is known that she gave Franz Marc one of her twelve illustrations of the Gospels and later others were given to Stravinsky and to Massine. To the end of her life she delighted and sometimes even embarrassed her friends by giving them splendid works of art.

In 1906 Goncharova was invited to participate in the Russian section of the Salon d'Automne, which Diaghilev arranged in Paris, a proof that her work was already considered to be of importance, although she did not accompany Larionov and him to Paris on this occasion, as has sometimes been stated. Later in 1906 she took part in the second exhibition of watercolours held by the Literary and Art Circle of the Leonardo da Vinci Society in Moscow. Among her subjects from this period were a number of pictures of the circus and of masquerades, possibly suggested by the work of Toulouse-Lautrec.

When she considered she had mastered all the light and freshness she had admired in the French Impressionists, she turned to more experimental work, 'shook off the dust of the West from her feet', as she declared, and found inspiration in her own country and in the East.

The decade before the Russian Revolution was one of intense activity in the Moscow art world. Larionov and Goncharova were among the prime movers of this

fig. 3 Mikhail LARIONOV
Tavern Still-life in a Major Scale
Whereabouts unknown. 1907. Oil on canvas
99 × 77·5 cm. Initialled bottom right in
Russian: M.L.

A small teapot standing over a large one which contained hot water was a feature of old Russia. Larionov admired all aspects of folk art and life and deliberately used crude subjects in his paintings.

outburst, when young artists were full of new ideas. They met, organized exhibitions of their work, usually financed by some rich merchant, then fell apart with violent quarrels, only to form new combinations with different objectives and other patrons. The first of these ephemeral groups was the *Wreath* [*Stephanos* or *Venok*] founded in 1907 by the brothers David and Vladimir Burliuk and financed through their father, the manager of a vast estate in the Ukraine. Larionov, Goncharova and Alexandra Exter took part in organizing the *Wreath*. This was followed in 1908 by the *Link* [*Zveno*]. More important in every way were the three *Golden Fleece* Salons. The first of these took place early in 1908 in a resplendent setting and included 200 works by French artists, ranging from the Impressionists, Post-Impressionists and Nabis to some of the avant-garde Fauves, who had created a great stir at the Salon d'Automne in 1905. This display of the latest developments from Paris must have been a revelation to young artists and a shock to the general public. Larionov and Goncharova were both members of the organizing committee and were doubtless responsible for the inclusion of the more advanced French works. It is not

fig. 4 Mikhail LARIONOV
Self-portrait
Whereabouts unknown. 1909. Oil on canvas
86 × 70 cm.

This laughing burlesque likeness is one of several painted by Larionov during these early years. It is presumably the one listed under the year 1909. Another is reproduced by Eganbury for the year 1910 and one is listed under 1911.

surprising that more violent distortion began to appear in Goncharova's subsequent paintings. This never took the form of direct imitation, it was rather a search for new forms of expression based on purely Russian experiences. The impact on the Russian artists in general was to appear in the second and third *Golden Fleece* exhibitions in 1909 and 1909–10. The rich colours of Gauguin, Derain and Matisse were more easily assimilated by the Russians than the classical design and slow, deliberate modelling of Cézanne. In Russia, as in England, his influence appeared later and continued throughout the 1920s in the works of such artists as Falk, Konchalovsky and Mashkov.

For Goncharova this was a transitional period, as she felt her way from the accomplishment she had attained in naturalistic painting to a more personal style. She had spent the summer of 1906 at Panino near Viasma and probably paid a visit to her relations at Polotnyany Zavod, where during the next two summers she produced outstanding work. Family portraits, including some by the distinguished eighteenth-century artists Levitsky and Borovikovsky, still hung in the drawing room, though little of the former splendour of life-style remained in the house. In any case Goncharova was more interested in the human outdoor activities on the estate. These provided her with innumerable subjects and above all she enjoyed complete freedom to paint all day. In 1907 she exhibited with the *Moscow Association of Artists* and at the *Wreath*, where her work was singled out as showing real talent. Her productivity was phenomenal, nearly sixty titles are listed for that year. Although not many of them can be identified, it is clear that she was making great progress. A powerful portrait of the painter Lvov combines the spiritual intensity of an icon with Cézannesque plasticity (M.C., 1972, p. 138). The two versions of *Larionov and his Platoon Leader*, one in Leningrad and the other in Paris (Plate 7), were painted during his military service c. 1909. A strong national trait, combined with personal handling, distinguishes her work from that of her contemporaries, who were bent on imitating the French. Action, expression and a peculiar rhythm, sometimes harsh and angular, enliven her country scenes. The use of strong colours, applied with Fauve breadth and freedom, and a transition from descriptive detail to broad simplification and expressive handling can be found in her paintings of this period (Plates II and III).

Interest in icons and in oriental art was growing at the time. Goncharova must have seen icons in the collections of Ostroukhov and S. Ryabushinsky and an article on Persian miniatures appeared in the *Golden Fleece* journal in 1908 (nos. 3 and 4) with reproductions of the *Baburnamah,* then in the Shchukin collection and now in the Museum of Oriental Culture, Moscow. Taste for Islamic art was gradually replacing the fashionable Japanese prints, although Goncharova herself had included one in her *Still-life with a Tiger Skin.* Young artists in search of synthesis and decorative stylization were looking to the East in order to escape from merely copying natural appearance. Subjects painted at Polotnyany Zavod include scenes of gardening (Plate 10) and field work, bleaching linen, hanging out washing, picking fruit and several pictures of boys fishing (A.C., 1961, nos. 93 and 94) and bathing (Plate 12). Primitive idols (Plate 6) and the wooden toys carved by the peasants during the long winter months were among the sources of her inspiration at this time. She came closest to the simplification of these carvings in the picture *Peasants Picking Apples* of 1911 in the Tretyakov Gallery, Moscow (C.G., 1962, plate 65). It was from this type of work that Malevich, who was in close contact with Goncharova at the time, went forward to produce completely non-figurative paintings.

A scandal was caused at a meeting of the Society of Free Aesthetics in 1909 when three of Goncharova's paintings, the *God of Fertility* (M.C., 1972, p. 138) and two nudes, were confiscated and a violent attack appeared in the *Voice of Moscow.* Eventually she was acquitted, thanks to the understanding and skill of her lawyer, M. Khodasevich, who owned several of her paintings.

Poetry, painting and music were particularly closely allied during the Futurist period. The poet Vladimir Mayakovsky was a student at the Moscow art school until 1913, when he was expelled together with David Burliuk. The Circle of Modern Russian Poets included Velimir Khlebnikov, whose work Goncharova was to illustrate, Vasiliy Kamensky, the poet-painter Elena Guro, and her husband Matiushin, who composed the music for the opera *Victory over the Sun* and painted completely abstract rainbow-like strips of colour thirty years before Morris Louis.

Although the Futurist movement in Russia was more concerned with literature than with the visual arts, Goncharova played an important part in it as a painter. Mayakovsky, who was one of the first to discover the art of popular Russian prints [*lubki*] and delighted in their fun and absurdity, found a similar joyousness in her work. The young rebels around 1910–13 were intent upon utilizing and combining all the art forms they admired, past and present. The Russian term for this universality was *vsechestvo* derived from the word *vse* [everything]. While the poet Khlebnikov invented new words or borrowed expressions from foreign languages to enrich his vocabulary, Goncharova did not hesitate to experiment with every kind of visual device. She rejected all academic conventions, not only in the choice of subject and composition, but also in the purely technical handling of paint. She would switch from the full brushstrokes of the Fauves to the smooth precise manner of the Primitives and at times even splashed or dabbed the colour on with a hard brush, regardless of form, a method used by Russian house-painters to decorate furniture and coffins. The painting of trays, a craft still practised in Russia, was another form of folk art she tried to emulate. *The Smoker* (M.C., 1972, p. 141) was described as 'in the style of painted trays'. The *Monk with a Cat* (Plate 15) is somewhat similar.

In 1911 Goncharova's work was widely shown all over Russia. She had more than twenty paintings in the second Salon of Izdebsky held in Odessa and was represented in the *Union of Youth* and the *World of Art* exhibitions in St. Petersburg, but the outstanding event for her was the *Knave of Diamonds* [*Bubulvy Valet*] exhibition, the first of three planned and organized by Larionov and held in Moscow in the winter of 1910–11, after they had left the *Golden Fleece*. Besides the two organizers, the new group included Lentulov, Mashkov, Konchalovsky and Falk, all of whom had been expelled from the art school for their left-wing views and unruly behaviour. A few French artists such as Gleizes, Le Fauconnier, Luc-Albert Moreau and the Munich group, Kandinsky, Jawlensky, Münter and Verevkina, were also represented. Twenty paintings

fig. 5 Artist unknown
The Archangel Michael
London, Temple Gallery. Nineteenth-century work from a seventeenth-century design. Tempera on wood 53 × 44 cm.

Elements of folk art are combined with the old tradition of icon painting in this nineteenth-century provincial Russian icon.

fig. 6 Artist unknown
The Feast of the Godly and Ungodly
Eighteenth century. *Lubok* [popular print] hand coloured on four sheets 74 × 56 cm.

This moralizing print in gay yellow, red, pink and mauve colours with touches of green probably inspired Goncharova's designs for *Le Coq d'Or.* The godly above are protected by an angel, the ungodly have devils prancing on their table.

СНЦЕ
ІС ХС
СІИАТРАПЕЗАНЕБЛА
ГОДАРНЫХЪЛЮДЕІПРА
ЗНОСЛОВЦЕВЪКАЩУНИКО
ВЪ СКВЕРНИГОЛЮЩИХЪ
СЛОВЕСЪБЕСОВСКИХЪ А
ДУША БЕЗБЛАГОСЛО
ВЕННА А НЪЕЛЪГОСПО
ДЕНЬѾВРАТИЛИЧЕС
ВОЕѾИДЕСТОАПЛА
ЧЕТЪ ВИДИТЪБЕ
СЫСНИ МИ
СИАТРАПЕЗАБЛАГОЧЕ
СТИВЫХЪЛЮДЕНДАДУШІ
ХЪНАТРАПЕЗЕСОБЛАГОСЛ
ОВЕНИЕМЪАНЪЕЛЪГОСПОДЕ
НЬПРЕТСТОИТЪНАДУШНХЪ
БЛАГОСЛОВЛАЕТЪАБЕСЫ
ПРОГАНАЕТЪ ХРИСТО
ВОЮСИЛОЮПОМЪРАЧАЕТЪ

were reproduced in an album with a cover designed by Goncharova (Plate 24). She sent in thirty-three works including five religious compositions and the pictures were hung in four rows. A Russian critic remarked that she had turned from the simplicity of sign boards to the complexity of *lubki* and praised the decorative line of her religious compositions. Larionov went further in his desire to discard French influence and turned to folk art, his pictures of soldiers and his *Self-portrait* (fig. 4) reflected the gay tomfoolery of the graffiti he had seen on the barrack walls.

In 1911 Larionov and Goncharova broke entirely with the French tradition and with those Russian artists who continued to follow it and formed a new group with the provocative title *The Donkey's Tail* [*Osliny Khvast*]. This was suggested by a newspaper account of a picture exhibited in Paris and praised by the critics, until it was discovered that some students had tied paint brushes dipped into various colours onto a donkey's tail and let him swish it about on the canvas. Larionov was delighted with the story, but violent disputes broke out between the new group and their former colleagues and it was in the course of one of these that Goncharova made her pronouncement about Cubism. She was described as a frightening woman in black with sleek hair and a fiery gaze. 'Cubism', she said, 'is a good thing though not altogether new. Scythian stone images and Russian wooden dolls were made in the Cubist manner.' No foreign works were included in the exhibition they held in 1912 and Goncharova occupied half the entire space with her fifty-seven paintings. They must have dominated the exhibition in sheer numbers and decorative splendour and included the *Peacock* series (Plate 19), the *Vintage* and *Harvest* series (Plates 20 and 21), *The Smoker*, *Peasants Picking Apples*, *Haycutters* and *The Woodcutter*. The police ordered some of the religious subjects to be removed on account of the frivolous title of the exhibition.

In 1912 Goncharova exhibited with the Blaue Reiter group in Munich and during the summer the Russian sculptor Boris Anrep, who was then living in England, came to Russia to select works for the Russian section of Roger Fry's second Post-Impressionist exhibition, which was to open at the Grafton Galleries, London, in December. Anrep remembered his visit to the studio of Larionov and Goncharova and declared that he had not seen any Rayonist works at the time. The Russian consignment arrived late and could only be included in the second edition of the catalogue. Goncharova was represented by the *Evangelists* (A.C., 1961, nos. 100–103), *The Grape Harvest* and *Spring in Town*. In 1913 Larionov and Goncharova organized another purely Russian exhibition entitled *Target* [*Mishen*] in Moscow which opened in April in the Polytechnical Museum. In addition to their own work, it contained paintings by Malevich, Shevchenko, Romanovich, Le Dantu, some younger followers and a collection of folk art, Chinese, Japanese, Persian and Turkish popular prints, icons, shop signs, Russian *lubki* and even the art of the pastrycook. All this made a strong appeal to the young because it was so unlike the photographic image of conventional painting. The *Target* also included works by the Georgian primitive painter Niko Pirosmanashvili (1862–1918), who had been discovered in the Caucasus by Le Dantu. A large collection of his works is now on view in the Tbilisi Art Gallery, Tbilisi, and a recent film introduced him to a wider public.

The catalogue of the *Target* carried a preface by Larionov in which he announced that a new style had been created, Rayonism, in Russian *Luchism*. This was the first exhibition to contain Rayonist works by Goncharova. *The Rayonist Manifesto*, signed by eleven artists, was published in *The Donkey's Tail and Target* almanac in 1913, which also contained Larionov's article on Rayonism, an article by the critic Varsonofy Parkin and illustrations of Rayonist works. The theory of Rayonism must have been evolved gradually and was the first step towards completely abstract painting, such as Malevich arrived at about the same time. According to this theory the eye does not see actual objects, but only the rays emanating from them. The artist uses the intersection of these rays in space to create new forms, selecting such combinations as he chooses and following the laws of colour. 'By this method painting becomes similar to music... Here begins the creation of new forms, the meaning of which depends exclusively on the degree of intensity of the tone and its position in relation to other tones.'

In addition to a few earlier paintings already mentioned, the exhibition included *Town by Night* of 1912. Its present whereabouts are unknown, but it was reproduced by Eganbury and was perhaps Goncharova's earliest exercise in Rayonism, although she described it as 'Futurist-Cubist'. Also at the exhibition were *Spring*, *The Mirror* and *The Factory*, all dated 1912, and several Rayonist compositions of 1913, including *Yellow and Green Forest* (Plate 31) and *Cats* (Plate 30). This early Rayonist phase did not last long, although Goncharova was to produce some abstract paintings again late in life, nor did it have a very wide influence on other painters, except on Franz Marc, who admired her work and introduced patterns of rays in his own paintings of 1913. Similar devices of rays or directional lines occur in the works of the Italian Futurists, notably Boccioni. Through Feininger, the ray-line became known in the United States and can be traced in the works of Joseph Stella and Charles Demuth.

There is little point in joining the controversy as to when and by whom the first abstract painting was produced. A tendency to eliminate subject and concentrate on form was widespread at the time and painters in several countries were experimenting in this direction. Goncharova's paintings were never quite as non-objective as Larionov's but, as Varsonofy Parkin said, if he invented Rayonism she confirmed it.

At the same time two entirely different new styles must be noted in Goncharova's work during 1913. One, a form of neo-primitivism begun in 1912, was possibly suggested by the works of Derain and Le Douanier Rousseau. Typical of this style are the tightly drawn winter scenes (M.C., 1972, p. 136) and the *Wood* [*Roshcha*] reproduced by Eganbury and described as 'contemporary primitive'. *Lubki* and naïve paintings found in Russia were a more direct inspiration than the French painters.

A preoccupation with modern mechanical inventions, a form of Cubo-Futurism, was the second development in Goncharova's art in 1913 and 1914. The aims and achievements of the Italian Futurists were certainly known in Russia before Marinetti's historic visit to Moscow in 1914, when he was violently attacked by Larionov for having betrayed his earlier principles and for his absolute rejection of the past. Larionov and Goncharova, as well as the poet Khlebnikov, were deeply interested in the old traditions of their own and eastern countries and made a special study of the poetic language and decorative art forms, which were still alive among the peasants. Goncharova's Futurist paintings include *The Railway Station* (Hutton, 1971, no. 30), *Linen* (London, Tate Gallery), *Aeroplane over Train* (Plate 32), *The Clock* (Berlin, Nationalgalerie), *Lady with Hat* (Paris, Centre Pompidou, Musée d'Art Moderne) and *The Cyclist* (Leningrad, Russian Museum). In these and other paintings of the period, Goncharova evolved a personal and highly colourful style. She did not hesitate to break up forms and rearrange their component parts, just as Kruchenykh would sometimes obtain poetic effects by jumbling the type used by printers. She introduced musical notation, letters and words, as they flash past in shop signs; she expressed movement by repeating the same form in several phases of its action and velocity by blurring contours. These Futurist devices were combined with a further breaking up of forms through the application of Rayonist principles, defining the rays emanating from different objects and thereby producing new shapes.

The intricacy of electrical machinery became an absorbing interest to her, in fact Tsvetaeva claimed that Goncharova was the first to treat it as having a life of its own. She was both fascinated and repelled, to her a clock was like a horse galloping along the edge of the world, a machine was not dead if it could move like an elbow or a knee and could stop. She said: 'The principle of movement in a machine and in a living being is the same and the whole joy of my work is to reveal the balance of movement.'

During the summer of 1913 Goncharova was not only painting furiously and evolving a new form of book illustration in collaboration with the poet Kruchenykh (Plates 25–27), she also designed some fantastic clothes for Lamanova, the smartest dressmaker in Moscow and started a fashion of painting on the human face. Larionov and his friends walked about the streets of Moscow with figures and animals painted on their cheeks and spoons stuck in their buttonholes to parody the aesthetes and draw attention to themselves. Finally, in August, when Goncharova was only thirty-two she staggered Moscow with her gigantic exhibition of 768 works held at the Art Salon, 11 Bolshaya Dmitrovka, which included her entire output from 1903 to 1913, except for three paintings, *Cats*, *Rayonist Forest*, and *Lady in a Hat*, which were at the first Stürm Herbst Salon organized by Herwarth Walden in Berlin.

fig. 7 Mikhail LARIONOV
Diaghilev with Leonid Massine and Three Dancers
Paris, private collection. 1915. Pencil 35 × 25 cm.

The dominant figure of Diaghilev is contrasted with the slender young Massine, whose first choreography to be performed was *Soleil de Nuit*, produced in Geneva in 1915 with sets and costumes by Larionov.

The following spring a smaller selection of 249 works was exhibited in St. Petersburg and was visited by 2000 people. The catalogue did not list the paintings in chronological order, as had been done in Moscow, and it included several works not listed by Eganbury, whose book had probably appeared at the time of the Moscow exhibition. These works may be assumed to have been produced during the winter of 1913–14, for example several religious subjects and the gaily coloured *Boy with a Cock*, now in the Art Gallery at Yerevan, probably suggested by a *lubok*. The last item on Eganbury's list

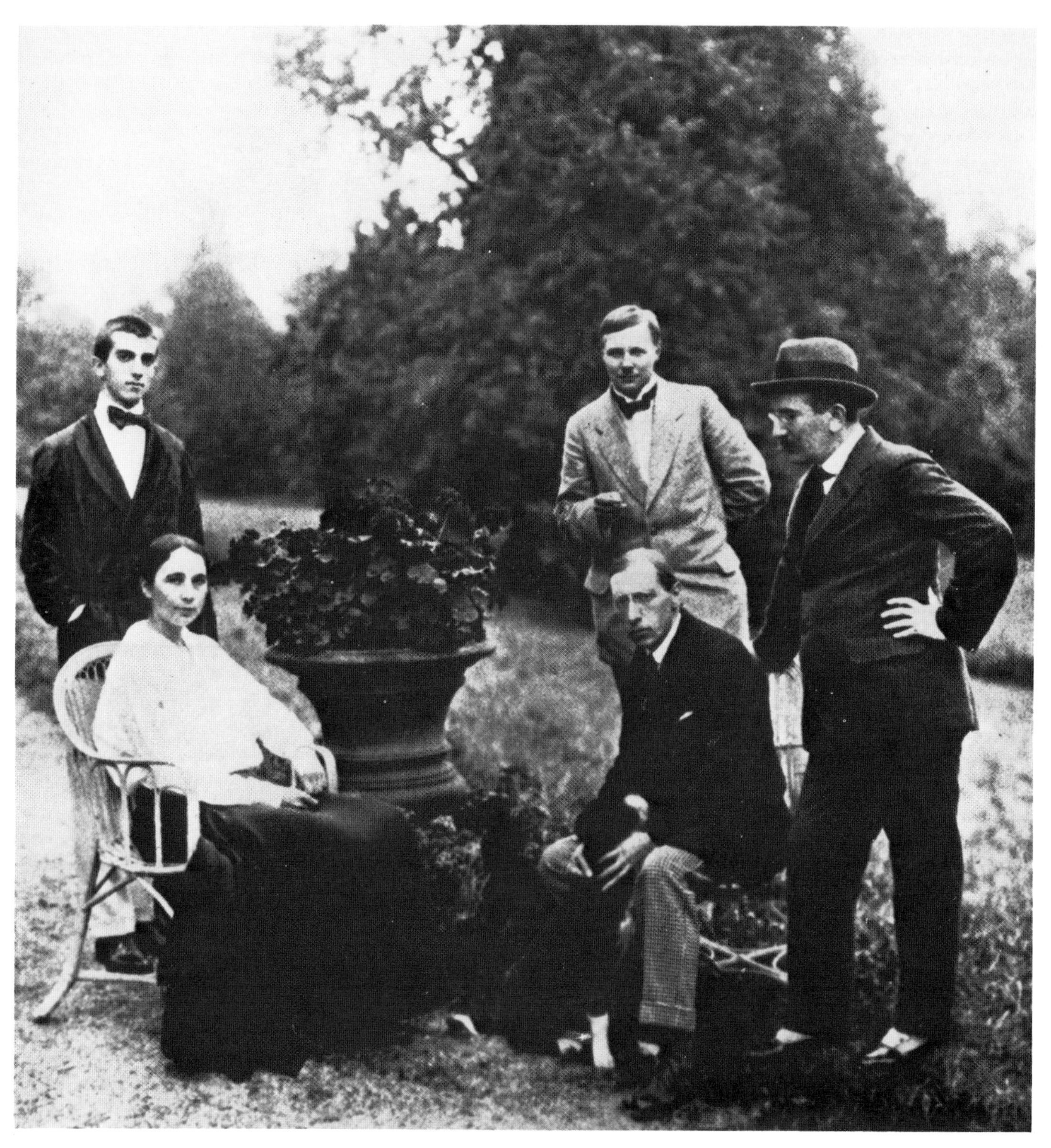

fig. 8

Photograph of Massine, Goncharova, Larionov, Stravinsky (seated) and Bakst in Lausanne, 1915.

can be identified with a *Still-life* with a bottle, jar of fruit and fish (London, Gimpel Fils). The original title was *Construction Based on Transparency* (*Theory of I. Firsov*).

In April 1914 Larionov, Goncharova and some of their friends organized a fourth exhibition in Moscow, which was accordingly entitled *No. 4* and consisted of Futurist, Rayonist and Primitive paintings. In the preface to the catalogue Larionov wrote that the artists 'had nothing in common except youth, similar ideas and the urge to press on in order to solve purely pictorial problems'. Goncharova does not seem to have sent any new works, as by then she was already working for Diaghilev, and for the next few years painting was to take second place in her work.

In choosing Goncharova as designer for the Paris production of Rimsky-Korsakov's opera *Le Coq d'Or* Diaghilev showed his usual artistic flair and foresight. He was always one step ahead of fashion by encouraging the latest movement in art, even anticipating the next craze. His devotion to art and his readiness to make any sacrifices in order to realize his ideals is one of the traits that endeared him to all who had the privilege of working with him. Goncharova herself described the blind adoration accorded him by collaborators in a manuscript, *Les metamorphoses de Noces,* describing the years she spent designing and redesigning the costumes and decor for Stravinsky's ballet *Les Noces*: 'This adoration explains to some extent, not only the artistic conscience with which every ballet was produced, but also the vibrant, over-heated, anxious atmosphere which reigned around this strange almost supernatural creature.'

Le Coq d'Or was not Goncharova's first work for the theatre. She had already made eight sketches for *The Marriage of Zobeide* by Hugo von Hofmannsthal for the Krafft Studio in Moscow in 1909. Her knowledge and understanding of theatrical requirements impressed Fokine when he and Diaghilev first went to see her.

'After all the terrible stories I had heard about the Moscow Futurists, I found myself in the company of the most charming, modest and serious people... I remember how earnestly Goncharova discussed every detail of the forthcoming production, how quiet, sincere and concentrated she was in all she said... I went away feeling thoroughly convinced that she would produce something unexpected, beautiful in colour, profoundly national, and at the same time enchanting. When we left I naturally spoke up in her favour, and I never had occasion to regret this. Goncharova not only produced marvellous scenery and costume designs, but displayed an unbelievably fantastic devotion to her work for *Le Coq d'Or.* It was very moving to see how, together with Larionov, she painted the entire assortment of properties by hand. Every object on the stage was a work of art... This was the beginning of our collaboration, which was resumed just as happily almost a quarter of a century later.

(*Protiv Techeniya* [*Against the Stream*], 1962).

In an interview with Franck Jotterand, Goncharova described the preliminary work she did in order to arrive at the perfection of the Paris production:

'I visited archaeological museums, where I was inspired by peasant costumes. I discovered such treasures as the magnificent rings of our Tsars and boyars. I had discussions with artisans. The Russian people have an innate taste for art. They have created folk melodies, which have supplied themes for all our great composers, for Stravinsky for example.

(*L'Illustré*, 24 September 1959, p. 65).

Fokine, in his account of the production stated that he too was inspired by old Russian toys and by the poses in Russian icon and mural painting when devising movements for his characters, just as Rimsky-Korsakov had used folk melodies and eastern strains in his music. All this gave an extraordinary unity and beauty to the performance. The subject of *Le Coq d'Or*, based on a folk tale and developed into a poem by Pushkin, is a humorous skit on effete monarchy. The artist Alexander Benois claimed to have been the first to suggest the novelty of presenting it as a combination of opera and ballet. The singers sat on raised tiers at either side of the stage and the action was danced and mimed in the centre by members of the ballet. The dancers loved the clothes designed for them because they were comfortable to dance in and made them feel they were looking their best. Goncharova chose a colour scheme of the utmost splendour and gaiety and tried out many variants for the scenery and for the drop curtain before deciding on the final version (Plates 37–44 and V).

Larionov and Goncharova came to Paris for the opening night on 21 May 1914 and the contacts Larionov had made with artists in 1906 were renewed. This was Goncharova's first visit to Paris and she was met by a delegation headed by Pavlova. One of the French critics present recorded that she was simply dressed, but had the carriage of a queen and greeted Pavlova with a courtly reverence. The season was a resounding success. In June an exhibition of Larionov's and Goncharova's paintings was shown at the Galerie Paul Guillaume. The well-known avant-garde critic, Guillaume Apollinaire, wrote a flattering introduction to the catalogue. He declared that she had accepted the influence of modern French masters and combined it with the subtleties of oriental art and with Rayonism, the latest expression of Russian culture. At the end of the season the couple went for a holiday to the Island of Oléron, off the coast of Brittany, and were summoned back to Russia at the outbreak of war. They returned via Italy, Greece, Constantinople and Odessa. Larionov was called up and sent to the front. He was severely injured during the retreat from East Prussia and after a spell in hospital was invalided out of the army early in 1915.

Meanwhile Goncharova was overwhelmed with commissions as a result of her Parisian success. The declaration of war by Germany had aroused an outburst of patriotism in Russia and many young officers went into battle with buoyant hopes, until defeats at the front and tactical mismanagement caused profound depression to spread throughout the land. Goncharova must have felt these contradictory emotions deeply, and was the first artist to give expression to them in her series of lithographs *Mystical Images of the War*, published by V. N. Kashin late in 1914. This spendidly designed set of fourteen plates combined elements of Rayonism, Futurism and Byzantine mysticism. The subjects include such symbolic themes as *St. George (Bringer of Victories)*, *The British Lion*, *The French Cock*, *Peresvet and Osliaba* (two Russian warriors who became monks and fought the Tartars at the Battle of the Don), *Angels and Aeroplanes* and *St. Alexander Nevsky* (Plates 34, 35, 36). Projects to decorate a church in the south of Russia and to design scenery for Rimsky-Korsakov's opera *Grad Kitezh* remained unfinished. The only work she was able to complete for the theatre was the scenery and costumes for Goldoni's *The Fan*, which was produced by Taïrov at the Kamerny Theatre, Moscow, on 27 January 1915 (Plate 45). These designs, together with some for *Le Coq d'Or* and a few religious compositions, were exhibited at the Lemercier Gallery in Moscow early in 1915.

By the summer of 1915 Diaghilev, who had been in Italy at the outbreak of war, was able to reassemble some members of his company in Switzerland and persuaded Larionov and Goncharova to join him. The journey must have been hazardous in wartime. While Larionov made his way from his home in the south by sea, Goncharova travelled through Norway, where she filled a sketchbook with views of lakes and mountains seen from the train. Then she crossed the North Sea to England and continued through France to Lausanne. Diaghilev had established himself at the Villa Belle Rive in Ouchy and Larionov and Goncharova stayed at a pension near by. Those were happy days of hard work, of planning future productions and of friendly contact with other members of the group.

Goncharova was working on a new ballet, *Liturgie*, which was to be performed by a small group of dancers because a full company had not yet been assembled. The idea of presenting a choreographic mystery had come to Diaghilev during his isolation in the early months of the war. The choir-master from the Russian church in Geneva arranged the traditional liturgical music, which was to be sung in the intervals between the dancing. The young Massine was working out the steps with the help of Larionov. It was his first attempt at choreography. While engaged on these designs, Goncharova studied Russian icons and Byzantine mosaics. The movements of the dancers were to simulate the stiffness of these formal images and all the personages were to wear masks. The floor was to be specially constructed to give extra resonance to the footsteps. The scene was to look like the inverted dome of a church with an iconostasis bearing the images of the Saviour and his Mother on either side of the Royal Doors. When the estimates for all this were totted up, they amounted to 4,000,000 Swiss francs and even Diaghilev could not take the risk of such expenditure. The ballet was never performed, the drawings remained with Goncharova, many were sold separately, so that it would be almost impossible to reassemble them again. Fortunately sixteen of the best costume designs were reproduced in a set of pochoirs (Plates 46–49).

Early in 1916 Diaghilev and his company went to Spain for a season of ballet in San Sebastián. The country left a deep and lasting impression on Goncharova and provided her with an exciting subject in the form of a new national image. Goncharova felt an urge to create in Spain, such as she had not felt since she left Russia, and for years afterwards elements of the Spanish scene were to reappear in her work, sometimes so stylized as to be scarcely recognizable. Probably the first exhibition of her Spanish pictures was at the Venice Biennale in 1920 and as late as 1939 she held an exhibition entitled *Espagnoles et Magnolias* at the Galerie Cadran in Paris. 'Painting and theatre work are indivisible', she wrote in a letter to the author, 'but painting is an inner necessity for theatre design, not the reverse.' Two new ballets were planned with Spanish

fig. 9 Mikhail LARIONOV
Dance Balance
New York, Museum of Modern Art (Study collection). 1916. Tempera 77·5 × 53·3 cm.
Signed below right: M.Larionoff 916.

This is one of several versions of the study of movement expressed in directional lines.

music, *Espagna* by Ravel and *Triana* by Albéniz (Plates 55 and VII). This encouraged her to study the intricacy of Spanish dancing, as well as the costumes (Plates 56–61). When it was decided to shelve these ballets, she continued to paint countless variations on Spanish themes and made some pochoirs of the backcloths she had designed.

After a brief stay in Paris, Goncharova followed the company to Rome in January 1917 and spent five months in Italy. She saw much of Picasso, who was in love with one of the dancers, Olga Khokhlova, and also met two of the Italian Futurist painters, Depero and Giacomo Balla, who designed ballets for Diaghilev. As a result of these contacts her style became more formal. Many artists were experimenting with Cubist, abstract and geometric designs during that period, for example Wyndham Lewis and Bomberg in England, the Futurists in Italy, Diego Rivera, Survage, Léger and the Purists in Paris. Angular, mechanically composed forms appeared in some of Goncharova's landscapes,

fig. 10 Mikhail LARIONOV
Design for a Curtain or Scene in 'Renard'
New York, Museum of Modern Art (Theatre Arts collection). 1921. Watercolour 52 × 64 cm.
Signed at lower left: M.L., M.Larionow; inscribed at right in Russian: Tale of a fox and a cock composed by Igor Stravinsky, Choreography by Nijinska, Decorations and costumes by Larionov 1921.

This design is an adaptation of Larionov's painting *Winter*, one of the four seasons he painted in 1912 and first exhibited at the *Target. Winter* and *Spring* are in the Tretyakov Gallery, Moscow, while *Summer* and *Autumn* are in Paris. At the *Target* there was also a section devoted to oriental and Russian folk art and children's drawings, which inspired the naïve style he tried to emulate in this series. The ballet *Renard* was first produced at Monte Carlo in 1922 and a second version, with choreography by Lifar, was produced in Paris in 1929.

such as the series of *Bridges*, painted in Rome in 1917 (Galerie Beyeler, exhibition catalogue, 1961, nos. 40 and 41) as well as in still-life and figure compositions. This tendency to geometric simplification appears to have lasted until the mid-1920s, while at the same time she was also painting in a more naturalistic style and making theatre designs.

While in Rome she exhibited with other Russian artists and later she and Larionov held a one-day exhibition of Rayonist paintings and drawings in the studio of Anton Bragaglia, who was to open his Casa d'Arte the following year. As no catalogue was issued, one can only guess which pictures were shown. The large collection of their work from the 1914 Paris exhibition had been seized by the Germans at the outbreak of war while on its way back to Russia and was only returned to the artists by Herwarth Walden at the end of hostilities. It is unlikely that they were able to bring much with them when they came to Switzerland in 1915, so presumably the works shown in Rome were recent productions. While probably small, the exhibition in Rome must have aroused interest, at least among artists, and an Italian version of the treatise on Rayonism was printed in Rome in 1917 as *Radiantismo* by 'Natalia Gonciarova e Michele Larionow', translated by Nina Antonelli..

The end of 1917 was a difficult period for Diaghilev and his company, for they were cut off from their homeland by the Russian Revolution and were caught by another revolution in Portugal. It was only thanks to the generous help given to them by King Alfonso XIII of Spain that they were able to survive and accept Oswald Stoll's invitation to come to London in 1918.

In the following year Larionov and Goncharova established themselves in Paris, in a fourth floor flat at the corner of the rue de Seine and rue Jacques Callot. This was to remain their home to the end of their lives. A few years later Goncharova acquired a large studio at 13 rue Visconti, off the rue de Seine, where she did most of her work and occasionally held painting classes.

In April 1918 an exhibition of their theatrical work was held at the Galerie Sauvage in Paris and in 1919 another was held at the Galerie Barbazanges. All this time Goncharova was doing urgent commissions for Diaghilev. She had designed costumes for the New York production of *Sadko* in 1916 and assisted Larionov with some of the costumes for *Les Contes Russes* in 1917. In fact Stravinsky maintained, in an interview with Robert Craft, that Larionov, like Oblomov, 'enjoyed a vocation for laziness and it was generally believed that his wife did most of his work'. There was undoubtedly give and take on both sides and it must be remembered that according to Vera Popova, who carried out many costumes and accessories for them, Larionov procured most of her commissions for Goncharova. While she was of a retiring nature and preferred to remain quietly in her studio, he acted as her impresario, spent his evenings at the Rotonde, knew everybody and went everywhere (T.L., 1971, p. 157).

fig. 11 Mikhail LARIONOV
The Fox (Disguised as a Nun)
New York, Museum of Modern Art. 1921.
Watercolour 51 × 34·5 cm. Signed above right:
M. Larionow; signed lower left: M L 921;
inscribed: Renard Opera National Paris 1921.
B. Nijinska *Religieuse.*

The Fox is one of the costume designs for *Renard.*

The success of the *Liturgie* pochoirs led to the production of another publication, *L'art décoratif théâtral moderne* of 1919, and two series of portrait drawings of dancers, issued in 1916 and 1926 (Plate 62). During the first years in Paris, Goncharova continued to illustrate books in a variety of styles and one of her lithographs (Plate 54), a stylized version of a Spanish woman, appeared in the *Bauhaus Mappe* (no. 4), devoted to Italian and Russian artists in the series *Neue Europäische Graphik 1921–23.* This is a work of the greatest importance in enabling us to date a number of rather similar paintings. It was evidently in the early 1920s that she painted the noble five-fold screen with elongated Spanish women and several groups of women with dogs, deliberately angular, almost wooden in appearance, with thick contours and geometric trees behind them (see Plates 53, 59 and 82). This simplification is carried still further in a series painted on mahogany panels with the wood left bare as part of the colour scheme and the whole reduced to a Mexican-looking rectangular pattern. The large and splendid group of *Bathers* (Plate 52) and the closely related *Autumn* at the Tate Gallery, as well as other paintings (Plate 51), pochoirs and lithographs, though given earlier dates by the artist, clearly belong to this period. In 1921 she made some designs in quite a different and entirely Western eighteenth-century manner for *L'Echarpe de Colombine* by Hugo von Hofmannsthal for the Russian theatre group Kikimora in Berlin (Plate 63). She also designed new costumes for the fairy tales in the last act of *The Sleeping Princess*, which was given as a separate ballet, *Aurora's Wedding*, after all the magnificent scenery and costumes by Bakst had been impounded in 1922 pending the settlement of Diaghilev's debts at the end of its short run in London.

Goncharova was always ready to experiment with new ideas and never allowed herself to get into a rut.

When she was about to strike out in a new direction with the austerity of her set for *Les Noces*, she told a journalist: 'The great fault with many modern designers for the theatre is that when once they find a formula, they stick to it and never get out again.' She was outspoken on the subject of eclecticism and outside influences. In conversation with Tsvetaeva she told her: 'I am not blind. I do not look at things in order to forget them... Is it permitted to remember a person and not an icon? You cannot forget a thing which has become part of you.'

In 1923, after years of delay and uncertainty, Diaghilev announced that he was going to put on *Les Noces* in Paris. The idea of making a ballet on the theme of Russian marriage rites was first suggested after the success of *Le Coq d'Or* in 1914. Stravinsky worked on the score while Goncharova was engaged on designs for *Liturgie* and other costumes. When she began to work on *Les Noces* she visualized it as a festive occasion with the peasants wearing their best clothes, but gradually she remembered the sad wartime weddings she had seen in Russia, when the groom was called up and the girl had to do his work in the fields. She decided to use the sober colour scheme of autumn, black, brown and white, a combination she also found effective in her Spanish paintings. In designing the sets for the ballet, Goncharova again may have thought of *lubki*, when she contrasted the stark interior of the hut with the carefully planned ceremonial of the movements. The choreography was by Bronislava Nijinska, who claimed that she was responsible for this austere interpretation of the theme, as the dancers could not have executed the complicated steps she had devised in the heavy costumes of Goncharova's original designs. Goncharova's fine outline drawings of groups of dancers for this ballet are more in the nature of choreographic projects than costume designs, for the two artists had collaborated perfectly in the end (Plates 65–70). *Les Noces* was well received in Paris, but in London the following year it met with complete incomprehension and even hostility from the critics. It was then that H. G. Wells came forward in its defence and described it in a letter to *The Times* as 'a rendering in sound and vision of the peasant soul in its gravity, in its deliberate and simple-minded intricacy, in its subtly varied rhythm, in its deep undercurrents of excitement, that will astonish and delight every intelligent man and woman who goes to see it'.

In the early 1920s Goncharova illustrated a number of books, painted a great deal, including portraits, landscapes, realistic subjects like *Le Déjeuner*, decorative paintings and completely abstract works (Plate 53). An important commission to decorate the house of the Russian conductor Sergei Kussevitsky at 8 rue Conseiller Collignon was a new experiment. The subjects were drawn from the world of Russian opera and ballet. For the grand entrance hall she painted the radiantly beautiful *Odette – the Swan Princess* rising out of the waves under the arch of a rainbow. Around her were ten other panels representing the four seasons, Lel the peasant boy from Russian folklore and some of the characters from *Le Coq d'Or*. In the dining room a frieze of half-length Spanish women attired in lace appeared half hidden amid magnolias (see Plate 83). The colours are delicate and the drawing is almost academic, without a trace of distortion. In 1924 when Kussevitsky was appointed to the Boston Symphony Orchestra, his house was let to an embassy. After his death the paintings were sold at Sotheby Parke Bernet in New York on 6 May 1970.

In these first years after the Revolution, artists who had managed to get out of Russia banded themselves together and organized a number of exhibitions. London had its first Russian exhibition at the Whitechapel Gallery in 1921, to which Goncharova sent forty-nine items, including a dozen *Espagnoles* dated 1916–18, some costumes for *Le Coq d'Or* and *Liturgie* and two landscapes. The following year Christian Brinton organized an important exhibition for Larionov and Goncharova at the Kingore Gallery in New York. To this Goncharova sent seventy-eight works, some of which had been shown at the *World of Art* in Paris the year before, including nine of her early Russian paintings of 1911–14, five Spanish subjects and flowers of 1916, three *Bridges* painted in Rome, as well as portraits and other subjects painted in Paris. Her fame was spreading world-wide. In 1923 there were exhibitions of works by Larionov and Goncharova in Tokyo and in Brussels. Even Moscow remembered their earlier triumphs and a retrospective of the *Knave of Diamonds* was arranged at the Tretyakov Gallery in 1927. Goncharova was represented by seven paintings, which now belong to the gallery. Prior to the season of the Ballets Russes in London in 1926, when *L'Oiseau de Feu* (Plates 75–79 and IX) was given, she held an exhibition of over sixty works at the Claridge Gallery.

In 1931 when Serge Chauby-Rousseau wrote Goncharova's biography for Edouard Joseph's *Dictionnaire biographique des artistes contemporains* he was able to say that she had been invited to exhibit in the great capitals and principal cities of Europe, America and Asia and that her work could be seen all over the world in public and private collections. But the tide was turning, the tremendous creative impetus was beginning to ebb and her work was losing some of its former vigour. The sudden death of Diaghilev in Venice in 1929 had been a shattering blow. Though she continued to work for other companies, it was never the same again. The last thirty years of her life were fraught with difficulties. She felt the separation from her own country more and more. Her work never recaptured the energy and joyousness of her youthful creations.

After Diaghilev's death a retrospective exhibition of ballet designs by various artists was arranged by Pierre

fig. 12

Goncharova photographed by the author, 22 May 1961. Goncharova sits on the edge of her bed, as she did when painting in 1961. One of her favourite early pictures, *In Church* (Plate 14), hangs on the wall behind her and a flower piece is on the right.

fig. 13

Larionov photographed by the author on 22 May 1961, his eightieth birthday. Larionov holds his painting *Spring 1912,* a typical example of his 'primitive' manner. The fat Russian peasant woman expresses fertility and happiness, with a bird on the right above and a pig on the left below.

Vorms at the Galerie Billiet in Paris, and together with Larionov and Goncharova in 1930 he produced a memorial volume *Les Ballets Russes: Serge de Diaghilev et la décoration théâtrale* (2nd ed., 1955). During the 1930s and 1940s Goncharova painted a number of flower pieces, the most saleable type of picture in the difficult years after the depression of 1929, some landscapes and repetitions of her Spanish subjects, but no imaginative works. At times her style came so close to her early Impressionist paintings, that some of these late works may have been exhibited as early ones. Now and then a landscape, for example *Marine*, and some decorative panels echo the angularity of her theatrical designs, but more often she painted straightforward French rural scenes, luminous and full of atmosphere. She was fond of spending the summer months in the South of France by the sea, where she relaxed and made drawings of rocks and trees. Her love of the country remained with her to the end of her life, though she was seldom able to enjoy it.

Fortunately the theatre situation improved gradually. Colonel de Basil reassembled the Ballets Russes de Monte Carlo and other companies came forward with commissions for Lithuania and America. Among the more important of her later designs for the theatre was *Sorochinsk Fair* after Gogol, in which her memories of hot summers in the Ukraine found expression in the placid country scenes she designed with rich floral borders encircling the stage (Plates 86–88). As Brian Reade pointed out (London, 1970), it is more naturalistic than her earlier work and 'in any case the hey-day of pioneering had passed and the atmosphere in which *Le Coq d'Or* and *Les Noces* had startled Paris had disappeared with Diaghilev'.

In 1932 Goncharova designed costumes and scenery for the opera *Tsar Saltan* for the National Theatre, Kovno. This was a subject after her own heart, as she had already illustrated a French translation of the poem (Plate 74). The following year she designed two items for La Chauve-Souris Company in New York, *Voyage d'une Danseuse* and *La Vie Parisienne.* In 1935 she again co-operated with Fokine in *Mephisto Valse* for the Opéra Comique in Paris. This was followed by new designs for the ballet version of *Le Coq d'Or*, produced at Covent Garden by Colonel de Basil in 1937. The following year Goncharova made her first and only attempt to recreate the western medieval scene in a romantic setting for *Cinderella* given as a ballet by de Basil with music by d'Erlanger. During these last pre-war years she was also working on a more familiar Russian theme for Massine's ballet *Bogatyri* with music by Borodin, given by the Ballets Russes de Monte Carlo at the Metropolitan Opera House, New York, in 1940. She continued to find work in Paris even throughout the 1939–45 war and the German occupation. At that time she was designing mainly for Kniasev, who had danced the Tsarevich in *L'Oiseau de Feu* and now had his own school and company. In 1943 he celebrated twenty-five years of dancing and a souvenir was published including reproductions of several of Goncharova's designs for his ballets (Plates 90–94).

After the war, in 1945, Larionov and Goncharova were able to revisit Monte Carlo. In 1948 her work was once again seen in London in the decor for *Il Barbiere di Siviglia* at the Cambridge Theatre and in 1949 she designed decorations and costumes for *Infanta ou Un Coeur de Diamant*, after a story by Oscar Wilde, for the Marquis de Cuevas's ballet company. Larionov was enthusiastic about this new patron, perhaps hoping for another Diaghilev. Unfortunately the enterprise did not last long.

The worst period in her life must have been after Larionov had a stroke in 1950, while he was in London with a ballet company. She came over to see him in the French Hospital, then in Shaftesbury Avenue, and stayed some weeks with her friends the dancer Catherine de Villiers and the Princesse Carlos de Rohan, who had a flat at 1 Lansdowne Terrace, Brunswick Square. When he was sufficiently recovered to return to Paris, Larionov had to spend eighteen months in a nursing home at enormous expense. Goncharova displayed extraordinary energy and began to sell their works to museums. Many ballet friends contributed generously to help him get well.

Although conditions became almost unbearably hard for Goncharova and she had to do without all but the barest necessities of life, her courage never failed and both artists were upheld by the growing interest in their early paintings, which had been lying stored in their studios and almost forgotten for years. A friend, Eugene Mollo, reminded Larionov of this possible source of income and brought Sir John Rothenstein, then Director of the Tate Gallery, to see him late in 1953. As a result two works by Goncharova and one by Larionov were acquired by the Trustees of the Gallery. Other museums in Europe and America began to take an interest. Works by Larionov and Goncharova figured in a number of post-war exhibitions showing the development of the modern movement and gradually the important part played by Russian artists came to be recognized. Their names were becoming familiar to a wider public, not only as designers for the theatre. Goncharova was encouraged to paint again in a more lively manner. She produced some new Rayonist drawings and paintings for her exhibition at the Galerie de l'Institut in 1956 and she left a series of tiny watercolour sketches of abstract compositions, some no larger than postage stamps, which, like Nolde's *Ungemalte Bilder*, were destined never to be carried out.

After the commission in 1954 to redraw the designs for *L'Oiseau de Feu* for Covent Garden and La Scala, Milan, had brought in more money, it was a relief for Goncharova to find a charming German girl, Anna-Maria Meyer, to come and look after her, giving domestic as well as secretarial help. This enabled the artist once again to devote her remaining energy to painting. On 4 October 1954 she wrote to the author: 'It is a sunny day and I feel light of heart. Now, having finished and sent off some time ago two big commissions, a theatrical one and four large panels to America, I am free and full of courage, that is to say, I am painting and thereby expressing my joy of life.' In another letter, two months later, she wrote: 'A spark of the spirit lives in us, it is connected with all spirit. It is divine. It is drawn to other, similar sparks. This is the urge to creation.' Tsvetaeva becomes lyrical when she describes Goncharova's attitude to everything that grows: 'All her green shoots and leaves – her very brush strokes embody the idea of resurrection, not the idea, but the tangible experience of it, here and now. Growth – that is what comes back to mind inevitably when one thinks of Goncharova.' She was always introducing plants and flowers, sometimes also birds and animals into her decorations, her book-illustrations and her paintings, spring flowers for preference, magnolia, cherry blossom, lilacs, daffodils, but also roses, peonies, thistles and occasionally autumn leaves. The very last painting, which remained unfinished when she died, was of daffodils and lilac.

Another subject that stimulated her imagination was flying. As early as 1912 planes had appeared in some of her paintings. When the first Russian sputnik went up into space, she painted a series of compositions on the theme of the cosmos. About twenty were exhibited at the Galerie Loeb in Paris in 1958. By that time she was so crippled by arthritis that she could not raise her arm to the easel, but would sit on the edge of her bed with the canvas placed flat on a high stool in front of her and she was just able to move her hand enough to paint. But her imagination was as agile as ever and she invented designs in which the infinite was given visible form, the mystery of the universe with planets moving in their orbits had become her theme (Plate 95).

When they were students, Goncharova and Larionov had believed in free love and only married in 1955 in order to insure that whoever survived should inherit the other's works. No doubt there were diverse attachments on both sides at various times, but apart from a few periods of estrangement, when they were not on speaking terms though living in adjoining rooms, they remained a most touchingly devoted couple to the end of their lives and full of admiration for each other's work.

For some years the Russian painter Leonardo Benatov, who was living in Paris, had cherished the idea of decorating with Goncharova the Chapel of St. Lubin on his estate at Chevreuse. In 1950 the project had to be deferred owing to Larionov's illness. Only two weeks before she died, Goncharova told him that as soon as she was a little better they could start the painting. Unfortunately neither this scheme of decoration, nor the earlier one to decorate a church in Russia was destined to materialize. She died of cancer on 17 October 1962 and was buried according to the rites of the Russian Orthodox Church in the cemetery of Ivry, near Paris.

Goncharova had conquered the West by her theatre work for *Le Coq d'Or* in 1914, but the importance of her painting, like that of many other expatriate Russian artists, was slower in gaining recognition and has come to be fully appreciated only in recent decades.

Bibliography

Bowlt, John E., *Russian Art of the Avant-Garde, Theory and Criticism, 1902–1934.* New York, 1976.

Buckle, Richard, *In Search of Diaghilev.* London, 1955.

Chamot, Mary, *Gontcharova.* Paris, 1972.

Chamot, Mary, 'Russian Avant-Garde Graphics', *Apollo* (December 1973).

Eganbury, Eli, *Natalia Goncharova Mikhail Larionov.* Moscow, 1913.

Eganbury, Eli, 'Goncharova and Larionov', *Zhar-Ptitsa*, no. 7 (Berlin, 1922).

Fokine, Michel, *Memoirs of a Ballet Master.* London, 1961.

Fokine, Michel, *Protiv Techeniya* [*Against the Stream*]. Moscow, 1962.

Gray, Camilla, *The Great Experiment, 1863–1922.* London, 1962; 2nd ed. 1971.

Khardjiev, N., 'In Memory of Natalia Goncharova and Michel Larionov', *Iskusstvo Knigi*, vol. V 1963–64, pp. 306–318 (Moscow, 1968).

Loguine, Tatiana, *Gontcharova et Larionov. Cinquante ans à Saint-Germains-des-Prés.* Paris, 1971.

Marcadé, Valentine, *Le renouveau de l'art pictural russe.* Lausanne, 1971.

Markov, Vladimir, *Russian Futurism.* London, 1969.

Osliny Khvost i Mishen [*The Donkey's Tail and Target*]. Moscow, 1913.

Parnack, Valentin, *Gontcharova et Larionov: L'art décoratif théâtral moderne.* Paris, 1920.

Reade, Brian, *Ballet Designs and Illustrations.* London, 1970.

Tsvetaeva, Marina and Sarabianov, D. V., 'Natalia Goncharova', *Prometei*, vol. 7, pp. 144–203 (Moscow, 1969).

Vorms, Pierre (ed.), *Les Ballets Russes: Serge de Diaghilev et la décoration théâtrale.* Paris, 2nd ed. 1955.

Mention should also be made of Goncharova's manuscript *Les metamorphoses de Noces.* A Russian version of this was published in *Archive Russe*, nos. XX–XXI (Belgrade, 1932) and a portion dealing with the production appeared in *Ballet*, vol. 8 (1949). The author is currently preparing an English version of the French text.

Principal Exhibition Catalogues

Paintings by Natalia Goncharova 1900–1913, Art Salon, Moscow, 1913.

Paintings by Natalia Goncharova 1900–1913, Art Bureau, St. Petersburg, 1914.

Exposition Gontcharowa et Larionow, Galerie Paul Guillaume, Paris, 1914.

Art Décoratif Théâtral Moderne, Galerie Sauvage, Paris, 1918.

Larionov et Gontcharova, Galerie Barbazanges, Paris, 1919.

First Russian Art Exhibition, Whitechapel Art Gallery, London, 1921.

Larionov and Goncharova, Kingore Gallery, New York, 1922.

Paintings by Natalia Goncharova, Claridge Gallery, London, 1926.

International Theatre Exhibition, Whitechapel Gallery, London, 1928.

Nathalie Gontcharova Oeuvres Anciennes et Récentes, Galerie de l'Institut, Paris, 1956.

Larionov Gontcharova, Galerie Beyeler, Basel, 1961.

Larionov and Goncharova, A Retrospective Exhibition of Paintings and Designs for the Theatre, Arts Council, Leeds, Bristol, London, 1961.

Gontcharova Larionov, Musée d'Art Moderne de la Ville de Paris, Paris, 1963.
Fauves and Expressionists, Leonard Hutton Galleries, New York, 1968.
Nathalie Gontcharova, Musée des Beaux-Arts, Lyon, 1969.
Russian Avant-Garde 1908–1922, Leonard Hutton Galleries, New York, 1971.
Retrospective Gontcharova, Maison de la Culture de Bourges, Bourges, 1973.
Larionov Gontcharova Retrospective, Musée d'Ixelles, Bruxelles, 1976.

(opposite)
I *Still-life with Shoe and Mirror*
PARIS, private collection. c. 1906. Oil on canvas 78 × 60 cm.

Although some authorities in Russia have suggested a later date of c. 1908 for this picture, too little is known about Goncharova's early work to be certain. The title, *Bunch of Daisies with Shoe and Mirror*, is listed by Eganbury under the year 1906, together with another very similar picture, *Bunch of Daisies and Hat*, which is also in Paris. The soft luminous colour suggests that the artist had been studying the French Impressionists and a similar light touch appears in some of her early landscapes.

(above left)
1 *Winter Night*
PARIS, private collection. c. 1906–07. Oil on canvas 77 × 60 cm. Inscribed below: Nuit d'Hiver Gontcharova 1858.

The date may refer to an old print upon which the composition was based, as suggested by the costumes. A dream-like other-worldliness, hazy bluish tonality and slender definition of form are features of Goncharova's early fancy pictures and point to the influence of *The Blue Rose* group of Russian painters, who held a single exhibition in Moscow in 1907. A partiality for costume painting had already appeared in the work of the *World of Art* painters, Somov, Benois and Lanceré. Several pictures of *Hoar-frost* are listed by Eganbury under 1904 and in 1906 we find a *Landscape from an Engraving*; evidently Goncharova was interested in the fashions of the past century at that time.

(above right)
2 *Woman with a Child*
PARIS, private collection. c. 1905. Oil on canvas 47 × 39 cm.

This winter scene, with icicles in the background and a peacock on the left, may be the *Woman and Child* listed by Eganbury under 1905 and is clearly related to the *Virgin with Icicles* of the same year (M.C., 1972, p. 135). The dating of these early works is very problematic.

(opposite)
II *Landscape at Ladyzhino*
PARIS, private collection. c. 1907–08. Oil on canvas 100 × 71 cm. Initialled below right: N.G.

The title of this picture indicates that it must have been painted on Goncharova's grandmother's estate at Ladyzhino in the province of Tula, where the artist spent much of her childhood. The painting shows the artist's full mastery of Fauvist breadth of handling and brilliance of colour.

4 *The Funeral*
LYON, Musée des Beaux-Arts. 1906. Oil on canvas 96 × 100 cm.

This sinister, dark urban winter scene, observed from an upper window, formed one of Goncharova's first experiments in using bold, dramatic handling. The difference in scale between the man leading the horses in the foreground and the row of people walking on the far side of the road may have been suggested by icon painting, a device which appears also in *Haymaking* (Plate 16).

(opposite)
3 *Tower of a Fire Station by Night*
PARIS, private collection. 1906. Oil on canvas 69 × 53 cm. Signed on back.

This street scene is similar in treatment to a number of early views of Moscow, for example *Red Houses* (Hutton, 1968, no. 21). They are expressive in design, but somewhat hesitant in handling. The rays of light round the street lamps anticipate the later Rayonist *Town by Night*, reproduced by Eganbury, but not located.

5 *Pillars of Salt (Cubist Method)*
PARIS, private collection. 1908. Oil on canvas 80 × 95 cm.

This and a very similar painting entitled *God of Fertility* of 1909 are both described by the artist as in the Cubist method. These comically monstrous forms with huge heads, inane smiles and no brains are without precedent, nor does anything like them occur again in Goncharova's work. *The God of Fertility* may have been suggested by a reproduction of Gauguin's sculpture *Oviri* or by his painting *Blue Idol*, now in the Hermitage Museum, Leningrad. Ancient Russian idols may have been another influence (Plate 6). Goncharova's claim to be the first Cubist in Russia was made at a debate in 1912 when Larionov and Goncharova left the *Knave of Diamonds* group. She declared: 'Cubism is a good thing, though not quite new. The Scythian stone women and the Russian carved wooden dolls sold at fairs were made in the Cubist style. These are sculptures, but even in France the point of departure for Cubist painting was the sculptured image, Gothic as well as Negro. During the last decade the first artist to work in the Cubist manner was the highly gifted Picasso and in Russia it was your humble servant. I certainly do not reject the work I have done in the Cubist manner.' The subject of *Pillars of Salt* is evidently an illustration to the Biblical story of Lot's wife.

(above left)
7 *Larionov and his Platoon Leader*
PARIS, private collection. 1909. Oil on canvas 104 × 99 cm.

This double portrait was probably painted while Larionov was doing his military service. Another version, in the Russian Museum, Leningrad, shows the two men wearing greatcoats. The blossoming tree appears in both pictures, but as the very youthful looking Larionov is here wearing a dark tunic and the older man a white shirt, this picture was no doubt painted subsequently. One of the paintings was exhibited at *The Donkey's Tail,* Moscow, in 1912.

(above right)
8 *Sunflowers with a Portrait*
WELLINGTON (NEW ZEALAND), National Art Gallery. 1908–09. Oil on canvas 117 × 109 cm.

Goncharova painted a number of pictures of sunflowers during these years. The head on the left appears to be a portrait of Alexander III and the picture on the right may be one of her winter landscapes with bare trees. The sunflowers, stuck into a watering-can, are losing their petals. Their seeds were a favourite food all over Russia and large fields of them were cultivated. The artist herself described her memories: 'Not when the plants were young, of a delicate green, covering kilometres of ground, nor when the flowers were the colour of the sun and turned their heads towards it, but a field of sunflowers during the harvest or even after, when the flowers left uncollected with blackened heavy centres drooped to the ground!' (MS *Les metamorphoses de Noces*). She evidently picked them in such a state for this picture.

(opposite)
6 *Stone Woman (Still-life)*
PARIS, private collection. 1908. Oil on canvas 130 × 146 cm. Signed bottom right: N. Gontcharova.

Also known as *Still-life with Pineapple*, this composition includes bottles, fruit and, in the centre, a small cast of an ancient Russian idol. A number of these images, locally known as *Stone Babas*, have been found and are now in museums in various parts of Russia. Goncharova probably obtained this cast from the Historical Museum, Moscow, or she may have painted it from drawings or from memory. She claimed that it was from these figures, rather than from Picasso, that she evolved her form of Cubism. It is significant that in the same year she painted *Pillars of Salt (Cubist Method)* (Plate 5). The print on the wall behind the figure bears some resemblance to *La Toilette* of 1907 by Matisse.

10 *Spring Gardening*
LONDON, Tate Gallery. 1908–09. Oil on canvas 103 × 123 cm. Initialled top right: N.G.

This is one of many pictures of gardening, bathing, fishing, bleaching and work in the fields painted at Polotnyany Zavod during the summers of 1907–1909. It is probably listed by Eganbury as *Work in the Garden* under the year 1908 and was no. 426 in Goncharova's 1913 exhibition in Moscow and, as *Spring Work*, no. 154, in her 1914 exhibition in St. Petersburg. The artist told the author that she never wanted to sell this picture, as it recalled the happiest time of her life. It does indeed epitomize the thrill of springtime, as well as the ordered rhythm of life and work on the estate, where the house stood on a hill and the white huts are seen below amid blossom. The women are carrying pots of tulips in boxes for planting out. Their blue silhouettes are broken by linear patterns revealing their forms, and white flowers are seen against the darker lilacs in the manner of Persian painting.

(opposite)
9 *La Jardinière*
NEW YORK, Leonard Hutton Galleries. 1908–09. Oil on canvas 106 × 74 cm.

A bowl of campanulas stands on a table covered with a richly patterned cloth. On the wall behind is seen a portion of Goncharova's painting *Women Bleaching Linen*, now in the Russian Museum, Leningrad. This subject is listed under 1908. Another picture of bleaching with two women standing upright was exhibited at the *Knave of Diamonds* in 1910–11 and is now at the Tretyakov Gallery. The rich reds and greens of the draperies and foliage set off the white patches of the wall behind, the bowls in front and the woman's blouse in the picture.

11 *Boys Skating*
MOSCOW, Tretyakov Gallery. 1908. Oil on canvas 48·9 × 70·5 cm.

This picture was bought by Ivan Morozov and went to the Tretyakov Gallery after his collection was nationalized. Goncharova's pictures of country amusements have been compared with the work of Brueghel, but the similarity is more in the choice of subject than in treatment. Goncharova never painted vast scenes with crowds of small figures. She preferred to select a few typical people and arrange them decoratively in a frieze-like pattern.

(opposite)
12 *Boys Bathing (Direct Perception)*
NEW YORK, Leonard Hutton Galleries. 1911. Oil on canvas 115·5 × 94 cm.

Boys Bathing was one of fifty paintings exhibited by Goncharova at *The Donkey's Tail* in 1912, probably as no. 74. The critic Varsonofy Parkin wrote in *The Donkey's Tail and Target* in 1913 that the 'first thing that strikes the eye is the mass of canvases by Natalia Goncharova. Without her and Larionov *The Donkey's Tail* would not exist. They are the ideological inspirers of the exhibition and their works, more than any others, realize the purpose of the exhibition. Her works can be divided into realistic works, religious compositions, scenes of peasant life and works in different styles, such as Venetian, Chinese, Futurist, Cubist, Egyptian. *Bathers* belongs to the realistic group, a powerful sketch in bright green and red, painted with so much expression that most of the works of the French school of this type, i.e. Matisse, will seem pale and anaemic ... I am not exaggerating when I say that in beauty of colour, in expressiveness, mastery and high tension of artistic feeling these works appear to be unique of their kind.' As there were several pictures of bathers in the exhibition, it is not certain to which these words apply, but they reflect the reaction of her contemporaries to her work.

(above left)
13 *Archangel*
PARIS, private collection. c. 1909–11. Oil on canvas 133 × 70 cm.

During the years 1909–11 Goncharova painted a number of religious compositions. It is difficult to identify them, as they are not precisely described in the lists and exhibition catalogues. They were inspired by icon painting and combine the noble tradition of Byzantine design with the coarser handling of the popular prints. The companion angel, facing left, is inscribed on the back: 'Part of a triptych *The Saviour*'. The central figure has not been located. Full-length angels are usually placed at the sides of the Deisis tier of an iconostasis, flanking the group of Christ with the Virgin and St. John. This angel wears green and advances with outstretched hands, the companion right-hand one is in white, with touches of red in his wings, his head bowed and left hand raised (A.C., 1961, no. 92). In her youth Goncharova had intended to decorate an entire church and had prepared eighteen sketches for the project, which was never realized.

(above right)
14 *In Church*
PARIS, private collection. 1910. Oil on canvas 102 × 72 cm. Initialled on back in Russian: N.G.

Also known as *Woman in Blue*, this picture was first exhibited at the *Knave of Diamonds*, in 1910 as no. 38. The artist had a special affection for this composition and it was hanging over her bed at the end of her life (fig. 12). She recorded the following experience in her MS *Les metamorphoses de Noces*: 'A woman clad in sky blue prays before a large icon with deep and empty eyes; the aspect of the two figures, the opposition of tones, the contrast in the expression of the two faces, the ardent faith of the woman and the abyss in the eyes of the image, struck me, and the memory of it keeps returning, even after I had made a painting of it.'

15 *Monk with a Cat*
EDINBURGH, Scottish National Gallery of Modern Art. 1910. Oil on canvas 99 × 92 cm. Signed bottom left: N. Gontcharova.

Like *In Church* this canvas may have been suggested by an episode the artist had seen, but is treated in an icon-like manner, with an arch round the figure and a hand blessing in the upper left-hand corner. The brimmed hat worn by the old man is unusual for a Russian monk. Men carrying bundles are seen in the background. The painting figured in Goncharova's exhibitions in Moscow in 1913 (no. 491) and St. Petersburg in 1914 (no. 4).

16 *Haymaking*
MOSCOW, Tretyakov Gallery. 1910–11. Oil on canvas 118 × 96·7 cm. Inscribed on the back: Haymaking.

In Eganbury's list a picture of *Women with Scythes* is assigned to 1909 and several pictures of haymaking to 1910 and 1911. The disproportion between the two central figures and the small cart and horse behind them, as well as the procession of tiny figures in the foreground, may have been suggested by icon painting or popular prints. In another painting of the same period, *Haycutting* (A.C., 1961, no. 95), the man with a scythe is twice the size of the two figures carrying sheaves in front. Similar disregard of conventions also occurs in the work of Chagall, who even turns figures upside down if it suits his purpose to do so.

17 *Winter. Gathering Faggots*
MOSCOW, Tretyakov Gallery. 1911. Oil on canvas 132·3 × 103·4 cm. Inscribed lower right in Russian: N.G.; and on the back: Winter Gathering Faggots.

This charming neo-primitive winter scene, painted almost in monochrome, was exhibited at *The Donkey's Tail* in 1912 (no. 31). The stars glittering on the bare branches of the tree give it a festive air and it was frequently reproduced for Christmas and New Year greetings in Russia.

18 *The Jewish Family*
PARIS, private collection. 1911–12. Oil on canvas 164 × 131 cm.

Two pictures of Jews were exhibited at the *Target* in the spring of 1913, one dated 1911, the other 1912. Five compositions of Jews are listed under 1912 in the 'primitive' style. The man in black is evidently an important visitor and the seated woman is comforting the frightened child in her lap. The artist was fascinated by their clothes, so different to the Russian peasant costumes she knew, just as the solemnity of their bearing differed from the carelessness of the Russians. A contemporary critic found a Spanish dignity in her Ukrainian Jews.

19 *Peacock in Bright Sunlight (Egyptian Style)*
MOSCOW, Tretyakov Gallery. 1911. Oil on canvas 129 × 144 cm.

This title was listed by Eganbury under 1911, together with *White Peacock (Cubist Style)*, which was reproduced and also published by Kruchenykh as a postcard, and *Peacock in the Wind (Futurist Style)*. An earlier *Peacock in the Style of Russian Embroidery* was listed under 1910. Five *Pictorial Possibilities on the Subject of the Peacock* were exhibited by Goncharova at *The Donkey's Tail* in March 1912.

(above left)
20 *Reaping*
OMSK, Art Gallery. 1911. Oil on canvas 100 × 93 cm. Initialled on reverse in Russian: N.G.

In 1911 Goncharova painted a series of nine pictures on the symbolic theme of the *Harvest*, as described in Revelation. This one illustrates the passage in Chapter XIV, verses 14–20. The curve of the sickle is repeated in a series of curves and crescents, suggesting rapid movement and flashing light. Two sketches for the composition are mentioned by Eganbury, as well as the final picture. Five, or possibly six, of the other paintings are in Paris and were exhibited in Lyon and in Bourges. They are the *Peacock*, the *Phoenix*, the *Prophet, Angels Dropping Stones* (Plate 36) and *Feet Pressing Grapes*. Possibly a rather similar painting of a lion may have been intended to symbolize *The King*. The eighth, *Woman on the Beast*, is in the gallery at Kostroma, and the ninth, the *City Flooded*, has not been identified. In contrast to the *Vintage* series of the same year (Plate 21), these paintings are treated in flat glowing colours without outlines.

(above right)
21 *Women Carrying Baskets of Grapes*
PARIS, private collection. 1911. Oil on canvas 129·5 × 101 cm.

This picture is one of nine compositions in a series entitled *Vintage*. A companion piece of men carrying baskets is in the Russian Museum, Leningrad, and others from the series representing peasants drinking and dancing are in Paris (A.C., 1961, nos. 104 and 105). The movements are angular and the extraordinarily rich colours are laid on rather flat with thick outlines in ochre. Tsvetaeva stated that the artist had never seen the gathering of grapes when she painted these pictures. The subject may be symbolic as in the *Harvest* series. The remaining five pictures of this set have not been identified.

(opposite)
III *Planting Potatoes*
PARIS, private collection. 1908–09. Oil on canvas 111 × 132 cm.

Planting Potatoes was first shown in the third *Golden Fleece* exhibition, Moscow, in 1909–10, when a whole room was allotted to Goncharova's work. It shows that the experiment with Cubism had not been forgotten, although abstract elements are combined here with observation of peasant life. Goncharova stressed the harshness of toil by the angularity of her figures and trees. This picture was shown again in the *Union of Youth* in St. Petersburg and Riga in 1910. Eganbury lists a sketch of *Peasants Planting Potatoes* as early as 1905. Although these early dates are not to be relied on, and the sketch may have been a different composition, the subject evidently interested her for some years.

22 *Bouquet and Peaches*
LONDON, Grosvenor Gallery. 1909–10. Oil on board 91 × 72 cm.

This painting is reproduced by Eganbury as *Bouquet and Peaches* of 1909, but listed by him as *Peaches and Vase with Flowers* under the year 1910, typical of the inconsistency and unreliability of even the earliest records. Comparison with the lilies in the *Self-portrait* (frontispiece) shows the development of the artist's style from detailed observation to simplified sonorous colour and deliberately distorted perspective.

(opposite)
IV *Elder with Seven Stars*
PARIS, private collection. c. 1910. Oil on canvas 147 × 188 cm.

This deeply mystical illustration of the vision of St. John, as described in Revelation I: 12–14, may have been intended as a sketch for the decoration of a church. The great arch, with angels looking down from the spandrels, is balanced by the curves of the golden candlesticks below. Instead of the white hair, as described by the Evangelist, the figure is clad in a gleaming white garment. In his right hand he holds seven stars to symbolize the seven angels of the seven churches of Asia.

2 ш

(above left)
24 *Winged Warrior on Horseback (St. Michael)*
Published in 1910. Lithograph on grey paper 7 × 5·5 cm. Inscribed above in Russian: Bubnovy Valet ['Knave of Diamonds']; below right: the artist's monogram.

Used as the cover of the *Knave of Diamonds Album* of 1910 this lithograph is probably the earliest surviving example of Goncharova's graphic work. The angular, compressed and very expressive design is inspired by icon painting and popular prints in religious books (fig. 5).

(above right)
25 *'The Game in Hell' ['Igra v Adu']: Cover Design*
Published in 1912. Lithograph 18·3 × 14·5 cm.

The Game in Hell was published by Richter in Moscow in August 1912. The text by Kruchenykh and Khlebnikov is a ribald account of a card game in Hell between sinners and devils. This was the first of Kruchenykh's books illustrated by Goncharova. The text was hand-written onto the lithographic plate and the authors declared that their writing [*samopismo*] differed according to their mood and could convey their feelings in a direct manner, independent of the actual words. Blake arrived at a similar effect of integrating text and illustrations by using etching. A second edition of this satirical poem was produced in 1913 with illustrations by Malevich and Rosanova.

(opposite)
23 *Ostrich Feathers and Ribbons*
PARIS, private collection. 1912. Oil on canvas 89 × 70 cm.

This picture, also known as *Street Wall*, was exhibited at the artist's retrospective exhibition in Moscow in 1913 as no. 627. Like the Tate Gallery *Laundry* it was probably inspired by shop-window displays. Braque and other contemporary painters were also fascinated by this theme. Twenty years later Ben Nicholson painted *Au Chat Botté* (Manchester, Manchester City Art Gallery) and wrote an illuminating account of the picture: 'The name was printed in very lovely red lettering on the glass window – giving one plane – and in this window were reflections of what was behind as I looked in – giving a second plane – while through the window objects on a table were performing a kind of ballet and forming the eye or life-point of the painting – giving a third plane. These three planes were interchangeable so that you could not tell which was real and which unreal, what was reflected and what unreflected'. (Tate Gallery, *Catalogue of the Ben Nicholson Exhibition*, 1969, p. 22). Goncharova's painting may also have been suggested by the painted signs at cleaners and dyers. These crudely painted, but decorative, sign boards were much admired by artists and figured in the *Target* exhibition as a branch of folk art. Liubov Popova painted a fairly similar theme in 1914 entitled *Early Morning* (Hutton, 1971, no. 86).

(above left)
26 *Man with Two Horses and a Cart*
Published in 1912. Lithograph on a postcard 9·3 × 14·5 cm.

The poet Aleksei Kruchenykh began his publishing career in 1912 by producing twelve postcards with designs by Goncharova, as well as twelve by Larionov and sets by other artists. Goncharova's subjects included her *White Peacock* and original designs such as this landscape.

(above right)
27 *'The Hermits'* [*'Pustynniki'*]: *Illustration of a Hermit*
Published in 1912. Lithograph 18·5 × 14·5 cm. Initialled lower left in Russian: N.

This *Hermit* is one of fifteen illustrations to Kruchenykh's parody *The Hermits* published in 1912. Like the illustrations for *The Game in Hell* (Plate 25) it combines popular humour with traditional Byzantine austerity. The naked hermit is reading a huge book while riding on a docile-looking cow.

(opposite)
28 *Portrait of Larionov*
UNITED STATES OF AMERICA, private collection. 1913. Oil on canvas 105 × 78 cm.

This painting was in Larionov's and Goncharova's studio in the autumn of 1913 when Fokine visited them with Diaghilev to arrange for Goncharova to design the décor for *Le Coq d'Or.* He wrote: 'Her paintings shocked me at first. In a large dark studio of a gloomy suburban house we were introduced to her work, for some reason by candlelight. The entire room was covered with paintings all facing the wall. One by one the canvases were turned for us to see . . . there was a portrait – the face almost a metre in diameter, I think it had only one eye' (*Protiv Techeniya* [*Against the Stream*], 1962). The portrait is unlikely to have been produced before the summer of 1913 as it was not included in the *Target* exhibition held in April and was first shown in the *No. 4* exhibition in April 1914. It has elements of Rayonism and the use of dabbing above and below the face. Though an abstraction, it remains a striking likeness.

30 *Cats: Rayonist Apprehension in Pink, Black and Yellow*
NEW YORK, Solomon R. Guggenheim Museum. 1913. Oil on canvas 85 × 86 cm. Signed lower right: N. Gontcharova.

Considered to be one of the most important of Goncharova's Rayonist compositions, this was first exhibited at the *Target* in April 1913 and then at the Stürm Herbst Salon, Berlin. For this reason it was not included in her Moscow exhibition, but was reproduced in the catalogue. According to the Rayonist theory the eye does not see actual objects, but only the rays emanating from them. The artist uses the intersection of these rays in space to create new forms, following the laws of colour. The last item in Eganbury's list is entitled *Construction Based on Transparency (Theory of I. Firsov)* and here this theory seems to be applied as well as Rayonism. The black cat's head appears at the top right and its feet below, a white cat can be discerned behind, its head on the left; their bodies appear to be transparent, perhaps suggesting the movement of the cats.

(opposite)
29 *The Weaver*
CARDIFF, National Museum of Wales. 1913. Oil on canvas 153·5 × 99 cm.

As this important picture is not listed by Eganbury, it was presumably painted after the book went to press, that is in 1913. It figured in the artist's exhibition in Moscow in 1913 (no. 765) under the title *Loom + Woman.* Goncharova's main interest was evidently the machinery of the loom and the electric light. A naked bulb swings over the woman's head and the row of lampshades to the left indicates the size of the factory. One can almost hear the noise of the wheels turning. The Futurist interest in mechanism is combined here with some Rayonist effects. The woman's arms are seen to move over the rollers, her body is only slightly indicated with a few blue strokes.

31 *Yellow and Green Forest: Rayonist Construction*
STUTTGART, Staatsgalerie. 1913. Oil on canvas 102 × 85 cm.

As this landscape was exhibited in the Stürm Erster Deutscher Herbst Salon, Berlin, in 1913 (no. 151) and reproduced in the catalogue as *Landschaft*, it was not listed in the catalogue of Goncharova's exhibition in Moscow, held at the same time. Another *Rayonist Forest*, reproduced in the catalogues of both the Moscow and St. Petersburg exhibitions, is similar to one in the Museum of Modern Art, New York. A number of pictures in both these exhibitions and in Eganbury's list appear merely as 'Rayonist Constructions' or 'Rayonist Interpretations' and are impossible to identify. Goncharova's Rayonist paintings were never completely non-representational and this is one of her most beautiful works in the Rayonist manner.

32 *Aeroplane over Train*
KAZAN, Art Museum. 1913. Oil on canvas 55 × 83·5 cm.

This painting is a typical example of Russian Cubo-Futurism, one of several in which the artist expressed her interest in railways and flying, then a great novelty. Effects of mechanization, speed and light are superimposed. Puffs of smoke are treated as solids and Rayonism helps to give movement and vitality to the scene, so different to Monet's Impressionist rendering of the *Gare Saint-Lazare*. The Russian Futurists were as keen as the Italians on dynamism, velocity, new forms of locomotion and the disruption of conventions, but they did not agree with the imperialism and militarism of Marinetti. Another picture of the same year, *Railway Station*, with figures hurrying along the platform, was in New York (Hutton, 1971, no. 30).

33 *Dynamo Machine*
PARIS, private collection. c. 1913–14. Oil on canvas 106 × 87 cm.

Goncharova was fascinated by electricity and exhibited several paintings on this theme at the *No. 4* exhibition in Moscow in 1914 including this one under the title *Dynamo* (no. 50), as well as *Electric Ornament* (nos. 53 and 54) and *Electric Lamp* (no. 45). This picture may also have been in the Paul Guillaume exhibition in Paris as *Dynamo Machine* (no. 36).

(above left)
34 *Mystical Images of War: the Archangel Michael*
Published in 1914. Lithograph 33 × 25 cm.

This lithograph is the seventh in an album of fourteen published in Moscow by N. V. Kashin in 1914. The subject of the horse prancing over flames is taken from a type of seventeenth-century icon (see fig. 5). St. Michael holds a trumpet in his left hand, a censer and a book in his right and a rainbow above his head links the two. In the time of trouble during the Polish invasion and civil wars this image had been used as a symbol for victory and was therefore particularly appropriate in the early months of the 1914–18 war.

(above right)
35 *Mystical Images of War: St. Alexander Nevsky*
Published in 1914. Lithograph 33 × 25 cm.

The last of the fourteen plates published in 1914 represents the thirteenth-century hero Alexander Nevsky, who as Prince of Novgorod defeated the Swedes on the Neva river and so became known as Nevsky. Later, in 1242, he won a still more resounding victory over the German Knights of the Teutonic Order on the ice of Lake Peipus. His last achievement was a diplomatic mission to the Tartars and he died on his return journey in 1263. When Peter the Great built his new capital, St. Petersburg, he had a great monastery erected there to enshrine the body of the saint, who became the protector of the city. In 1750 the Empress Elizabeth had a splendid sarcophagus, surrounded by trophies, made for the shrine from the first silver quarried from the mines at Kolyvan. Although this was moved to the Hermitage Museum after the Revolution, Alexander Nevsky is still honoured as a national hero and was the subject of Eisenstein's famous 1938 film.

36 *Mystical Images of War: Angels Dropping Stones over a City*
Published in 1914. Lithograph 33 × 25 cm.

The apocalyptic theme of angels dropping stones over a condemned city (Revelation XVIII: 21) had already been treated by the artist as one of her nine compositions in the *Harvest* in 1911 (Maison de la Culture de Bourges, exhibition catalogue, 1973, no. 26). In 1914 it acquired a wartime significance.

(opposite top)
37 *Project for a Curtain*
PARIS, private collection. 1913–14. Gouache 52·5 × 68·5 cm. Signed lower left: N. Gontcharowa.

This design is composed of Russian folk art elements, carved window surrounds, a siren, cocks and details of houses. It has been variously described as a project for *Le Coq d'Or* or the early design for *Les Noces.*

(opposite bottom)
38 *'Le Coq d'Or': Project for a Curtain*
PARIS, collection of Evelyne Cournand. Pencil and watercolour 46 × 61 cm.

This design may have been the first idea for a curtain or prologue to the 1914 production of *Le Coq d'Or*, which was never used. At a later stage Goncharova placed the same dancers and musicians in front of a banqueting scene with King Dodon and his sons, as well as his nurse, his general, the Astrologer and the Queen of Shemakhan seated at a round table (see Plate 39). This drawing was unfinished; only the foreground is coloured. In the end neither project was used, but the drawings are among Goncharova's masterpieces.

41 *'Le Coq d'Or': Design for the Battlefield*
EDINBURGH, Scottish National Gallery of Modern Art. 1913. Watercolour 65 × 98 cm. Signed at bottom centre: N. Gontcharova, 'Coq d'Or'; signed on the right in Russian: N. Goncharova 1913.

This bare and gloomy backdrop for Act II of *Le Coq d'Or* is in dramatic contrast to the gaily coloured and playful absurdity of the palace scenes in Acts I and III. When King Dodon hears that his two sons have been killed, he sets out to visit the battlefield. While he is lamenting, the magical tent of the Queen of Shamakhan appears, he forgets his grief and carries her off to his palace.

(opposite top)
39 *'Le Coq d'Or': Project for a Curtain*
LONDON, Victoria and Albert Museum. 1914. Watercolour 53·4 × 73·6 cm. Signed bottom right: N. Gontcharowa; signed above: N. Gontcharova.

This project appears to be an elaboration of the unfinished sketch (Plate 38). It shows the setting for the banqueting scene without any figures. The idea may have been suggested by a Russian *lubok* (fig. 6), or a medieval manuscript. The original *lubok* is gaily coloured in red, yellow and pink with touches of green and mauve. A still later version of the project was exhibited at the Diaghilev exhibition in Edinburgh and London in 1955 and showed all the principal characters seated at the table, groups of women standing at the sides and the musicians and dancing men in front. The colour scheme of red, which is synonymous with beauty in Russian, orange, yellow and touches of blue, green and pink expresses the festive spirit of Russian folk art and was a revelation to the Western world. The only figures in this drawing are the spectators in the windows at the sides. A rich border of stylized flowers surrounds the scene.

(opposite bottom)
40 *'Le Coq d'Or': Design for Act 1*
Whereabouts unknown.

The subject *Le Coq d'Or,* based on a folk tale and developed into a poem by Pushkin, is a humorous skit on effete monarchy. When the curtain rises the king is asleep and his nurse gets him up. He hears that his kingdom is beset by enemies. When an astrologer offers him a golden cockerel who will alert him to impending danger, King Dodon offers him anything he asks for as a reward. The first time the cock crows the king sends his two sons into battle, the second time he goes himself. The palace is a typical Russian turreted kremlin and immediately evokes the gay world of Russian folk tales and toys. In 1914 the opera was acted by dancers and the singers sat on tiered benches at the sides. In 1937 it was revived as a ballet by Fokine for Colonel de Basil and Goncharova made some fresh drawings. The actual backcloth and arch for this scene and some of the costumes were sold at Sotheby's on 17 July 1968.

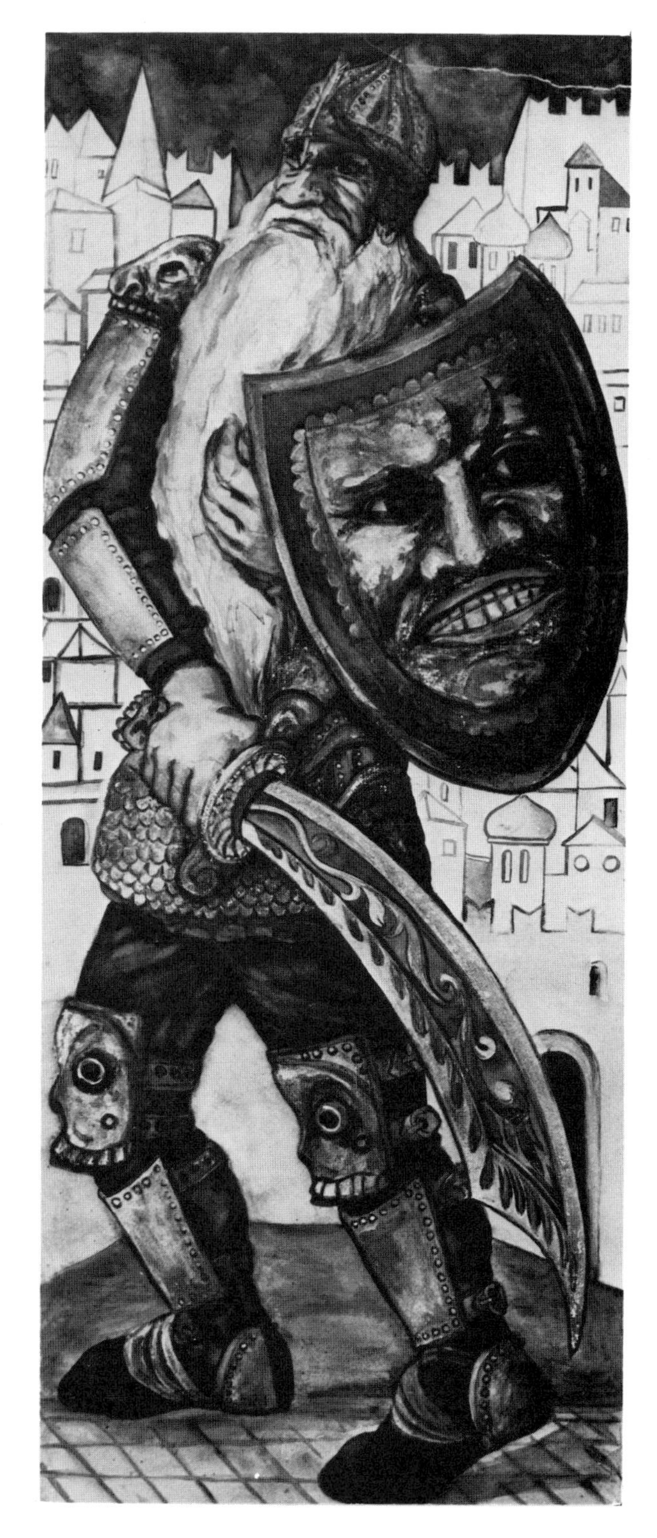

(above left and right)
42 and 43 *'Le Coq d'Or': Costumes for Prince Gvidon and General Polkan*
PARIS, collection of Evelyne Cournand. 1914. Gouache 78·5 × 33·5 cm and 80 × 45 cm.

Both men carry shields with threatening faces on them, but their poses indicate their military ineffectiveness. These and other figures from *Le Coq d'Or* were used again for the decorative panels painted in the early 1920s for Kussevitsky's house in Paris.

(opposite)
V *'Le Coq d'Or': Costume for a Russian Woman*
PARIS, private collection. 1914. Gouache 38 × 27 cm.

The design is typical of the gay colour scheme, based on red, yellow, orange and blue, which took Paris by storm in 1914. The original back-drops and costumes made for the ballet version produced by de Basil in 1937 were sold at Sotheby's on 17 July 1968. It is not always easy to distinguish between the drawings made for the first Paris production of 1914 and those made by the artist for the 1937 revival, but this and the set of ten costume designs at the Victoria and Albert Museum, London, certainly date from the original production.

44 *Dancing Muzhik*
PARIS, private collection. 38·5 × 27·5 cm. Signed on the back.

Dancing Muzhik was evidently a drawing for the 1914 production of *Le Coq d'Or* as it was exhibited at the Whitechapel Gallery, London, in 1928, with other designs from the opera.

(opposite top)
VI *The Rowers*
LONDON, collection of A. J. Richards. 1912. Oil on canvas 54 × 116 cm. Signed bottom right: N. Gontcharova.

This is probably the picture listed by Eganbury under the year 1912 as *Rowers' Race*. It was no. 626 in Goncharova's Moscow exhibition in 1913. The colour scheme of orange boats and oars against the deep blue, green and white water sets off the bold diagonal design. An inscription on the back of the canvas: 'peint en Russia en 1906 N. Gontcharova', is evidently of later date and inaccurate. It was probably added when the picture was sold in Paris.

(opposite bottom)
VII *'Triana': Project for a Backcloth*
PARIS, private collection. 1916. Gouache on cardboard 55 × 77 cm. Signed below right: N. Gontcharova.

Triana was one of the ballets on Spanish themes with music by Spanish composers, conceived by Diaghilev as a tribute to King Alfonso XIII, who was an ardent admirer of the Ballets Russes and attended their performances regularly in San Sebastián and Madrid in 1916. The music was composed by Albéniz. Goncharova worked on the costumes the following year in Rome, but the ballet was never produced. There are still traces of Rayonism in the background chimneys and smoke.

45 *'The Fan': Design*
MOSCOW, Bakhrushin Central Theatre Museum. 1914–15. Gouache and watercolour
49·6 × 58·5 cm.

Goldoni's play *The Fan* was produced by Taïrov at the Kamerny Theatre, Moscow on 27 January 1915. Goncharova had made a careful study of eighteenth-century costume and architecture, but had not yet been to Italy. Marina Tsvetaeva, who saw the play, could only remember the dazzling beauty of the blossoming apple tree in the centre, which unfortunately does not show up in the reproduction.

(above left)
46 *'Liturgie': Figure of Christ*
Published in 1915. Pochoir 63·5 × 38 cm.

When it was decided not to produce *Liturgie* Goncharova used some of her designs for an album of sixteen pochoirs, of which this is one. The *Liturgie* pochoirs were issued in Paris in 1915. They included a mourning Virgin, two angels, a priest, a Roman soldier, a king, a shepherd and several apostles. Some, like this one, are enclosed in an arch, others have a suggestion of a tree or building in the background.

(above right)
47 *'Liturgie': Six-winged Cherubim*
Published in 1915. Pochoir 75 × 55·5 cm.

Designed as a costume for *Liturgie*, the *Six-winged Cherubim* was also used as a pochoir in the album published in 1915.

(above left)
48 *'Liturgie': Costume for One of the Magi*
PARIS, private collection. 1915. Watercolour, collage and tinsel 60 × 47 cm.

Every line of this drawing emphasizes the urgency of the man's forward movement. The ornaments stuck on over the watercolour help to give the costume an exotic appearance. This subject was not included in the set of pochoirs. A drawing of a bearded king in a similar technique, but facing the other way, is in the Scottish National Gallery of Modern Art, Edinburgh.

(above right)
49 *'Liturgie': the Apostle Judas*
RICHMOND (VIRGINIA), Virginia Museum of Fine Arts (Council Graphic Arts Fund). 1915. Pencil and black crayon 56 × 41 cm. Signed bottom right: N. Gontcharova.

This drawing emphasizes the troubled expression and grasping hand of Judas and is closely followed by the pochoir which was published when the projected ballet *Liturgie* had to be abandoned. A number of drawings were made for the project and there is a sketch-book of them in the Victoria and Albert Museum. Goncharova had studied the poses and draperies in Byzantine and Russian icons and in an article published in Vorms's *Les Ballets Russes: Serge de Diaghilev et la décoration théâtrale* she wrote: 'Theatrical costume represents the particular sign, the significant detail, which helps to explain the character and his possibilities; it helps to create the desired atmosphere, even before the performer speaks, sings or dances. It creates a grotesque effect by contrast, supports the harmony, complicates or simplifies the gestures or the meaning of speech. It is precisely in this that the essential relationship between costume and movement, between costume and the Word manifest themselves.'

50 *Project for a Curtain or Backcloth*
GARRISON (NEW YORK), by permission of Mr. Dan Flavin. Watercolour and gouache 65 × 84 cm.

Although previously described as a design for *Rhapsodie Espagnole*, the 1916 ballet with music by Ravel which was never produced, this composition has many elements typical of Goncharova's work during her last year in Russia, such as letters, figures and musical notation, flowering trees and intersecting rays. The toys painted on the houses look unmistakably Russian. It may be a project for *Le Coq d'Or* or *Les Noces* or Fokine's ballet *Russian Toys* given at the Palace Theatre, New York, in 1921.

51 *Flowers and Frames*
NEW YORK, Leonard Hutton Galleries. c. 1917–23. Oil on canvas 65 × 54 cm. Signed upper left: N. Gontcharova.

This composition appears to make use of reflections in a mirror and views through a window. It has sometimes been called *Rayonist Flowers*, but there does not seem to be any use of Rayonism in the painting. The colour scheme of browns and blacks is typical of the early 1920s and recalls the later Spanish subjects. The technique resembles that used in *Peacocks* (Plate VIII).

(opposite)
52 *Bathers*
LONDON, Grosvenor Gallery. c. 1917–23. Oil on canvas 230 × 153 cm. Signed below right: N. Gontcharova.

The style of this composition is closely related in colour and form to *Autumn* in the Tate Gallery, London, and is clearly a further development of the Bauhaus print (Plate 54). Another definitely dated design with similar forms is the poster for the Bal Travesti held in the Salle Bullier on 23 February 1923 (T.L., 1971, p. 138). There is a severe beauty in all these paintings, the rhythm of the design always justifies the simplification of form. The influence of Picasso and other Cubist painters was no doubt responsible for this brief phase of Goncharova's work.

(above left)
53 *Abstract Figure*
Whereabouts unknown. c. 1920–23. Oil on canvas 105 × 78 cm. Signed lower right: N. Gontcharova; inscribed on back: A Madame Florence Bank amicalement.

While this angular figure is similar in treatment to the Bauhaus print (Plate 54), the actual pose seems to be that of the Swan Princess in the illustration to *Tsar Saltan* (Plate 74). It appears that the artist was working in a realistic and decorative style and at the same time experimenting with abstraction. Perhaps the one was a natural reaction to the other.

(above right)
54 *Half-length of a Woman*
1922–23. Lithograph in black, blue and yellow 49·5 × 33·9 cm. Signed below left on the stone and again below: N. Gontcharova.

This lithograph was published in the fourth set of *Bauhausdrücke, Neue Europäische Graphik* [*New European Graphics*], which was devoted to Russian and Italian artists. The series was begun in 1921 with a set of German graphics, the second set, planned to represent French art, never materialized, the third was again devoted to German art. This print is of fundamental importance in dating Goncharova's paintings. She would certainly not have used a ten-year-old composition to represent her in a series entitled *New European Graphics.* Therefore, a number of paintings in a Cubist and near-abstract style must be dated in the early 1920s, though they have been given much earlier dates in a number of exhibitions.

(opposite)
55 *The Orange Seller*
PARIS, private collection. c. 1916–18. Oil on canvas 131 × 97 cm. Signed lower left: N. Gontcharova.

Although dated 1912–13 in the 1961 Arts Council exhibition catalogue, this oil was clearly painted after the artist's visit to Spain and bears no resemblance to any of her Russian paintings. A photograph of this picture in the Witt Library is inscribed in Goncharova's hand: 'Costume pour Albéniz 1916', but at the 1921 Russian Exhibition at the Whitechapel Art Gallery *The Orange Seller* was dated 1918 in the catalogue. Perhaps *The Orange Seller* was intended for one of the 'figurants' described in Vorms: 'Costume and décor can be related to one another sometimes in a highly complex manner. For example, there is nothing to prevent the designer from inventing new forms of scenic properties, which fall between traditional costume and scenery. The projects for *Espagna* and *Triana* designed in 1916 envisaged painted and cut-out figures, larger and smaller than real life, fixed on mobile chassis, which could slide from side to side, parallel to the footlights. The dancers in ordinary costume could move sometimes in front and sometimes behind these mobile chassis, and their evolutions on one or other plane produced effects of unusual perspective'.

(above left)
56 *'Rhapsodie Espagnole': Spanish Dancer with a Shawl and Comb*
PARIS, private collection. 1916. Gouache 65·5 × 43 cm. Signed at top left: N. Gontcharowa.

In this costume design for *Rhapsodie Espagnole*, the nose, eye and mouth are shown in two positions to suggest rapid movement. In *Spanish Woman with a Fan* (Plate 61) the left eye is seen to the right of the head.

(above right)
57 *'Rhapsodie Espagnole': Spanish Costume for Male Dancer*
PARIS, private collection. 1916. Gouache 66 × 44 cm. Signed bottom right: N. Gontcharowa.

The pose shows close observation of typical Spanish movements.

(above left)
58 *Portrait of Tamara Karsavina*
VIENNA, Nationalbibliothek. 1920–25. Charcoal on paper 56·9 × 77·5 cm. Signed top right: N. Gontcharova.

A portrait of Karsavina was included in the pochoirs *Portraits théâtraux* of 1916, but the style of the Vienna drawing seems to point to the early 1920s. The head-dress and elongated arms recall the Spanish screen and the ticket for the Bal Banal (Plate 59).

(above right)
59 *Two Spanish Women*
1923. Print in brown and grey on buff paper 30·5 × 15·7 cm. with stubs. Signed bottom left: N. Gontcharova 923.

The figures on this ticket for the Bal Banal, organized by the *Union of Russian Artists* in Paris and held at the Salle Bullier on 14 March 1924, resemble the second and third in the large screen painted at about the same time (M. C., 1972, p. 101). All the tickets for this ball were printed with the same design, but on different coloured paper, according to the price and the location in the Salle Bullier.

(above left)
60 *Photograph of a Dancer Wearing One of Goncharova's Costumes*

(above right)
61 *'Rhapsodie Espagnole': Spanish Woman with a Fan*
PARIS, private collection. 1916. Gouache 65 × 43·5 cm. Signed upper left: N. Gontcharova.

The ballet *Rhapsodie Espagnole* was rehearsed but never produced. The fan and the enormous flowers and fringe of the shawl in this costume design have been deliberately exaggerated, as can be seen by a comparison with the photograph of a dancer wearing one of Goncharova's costumes (Plate 60), reproduced from Fülop-Miller and Gregor, *The Russian Theatre* (London, 1930).

(left)
62 *Portrait of Leonid Massine*
c. 1916. Pochoir. Initialled lower right: N.G.

The first set of fourteen *Portraits théâtraux*, including this portrait of Massine, was drawn in Lausanne and San Sebastián and published by La Cible, Paris, in an edition of thirty-five copies in 1916. Rayonist elements appear in many of these portraits.

63 *'L'Echarpe de Colombine': Design for an Interior*
LONDON, Grosvenor Gallery. 1922. Watercolour 35 × 43 cm. Signed at bottom right: N. Gontcharova.

The pantomime by Fedorova based on the play by Hugo von Hofmannsthal was produced by Tchebotarev and Vermel at the Kikimora Theatre, Berlin, in 1922. Goncharova designed the scenery and costumes.

64 *Russian Costume Designed for Anna Pavlova*
LONDON, Victoria and Albert Museum. c. 1925. Watercolour, gouache, gold and silver paint 65 × 51 cm. Signed bottom left: N. Gontcharova; inscribed on the back: Pour Pavlova [with the artist's name and address].

This very elaborate costume appears never to have been used by Pavlova. The side view of the

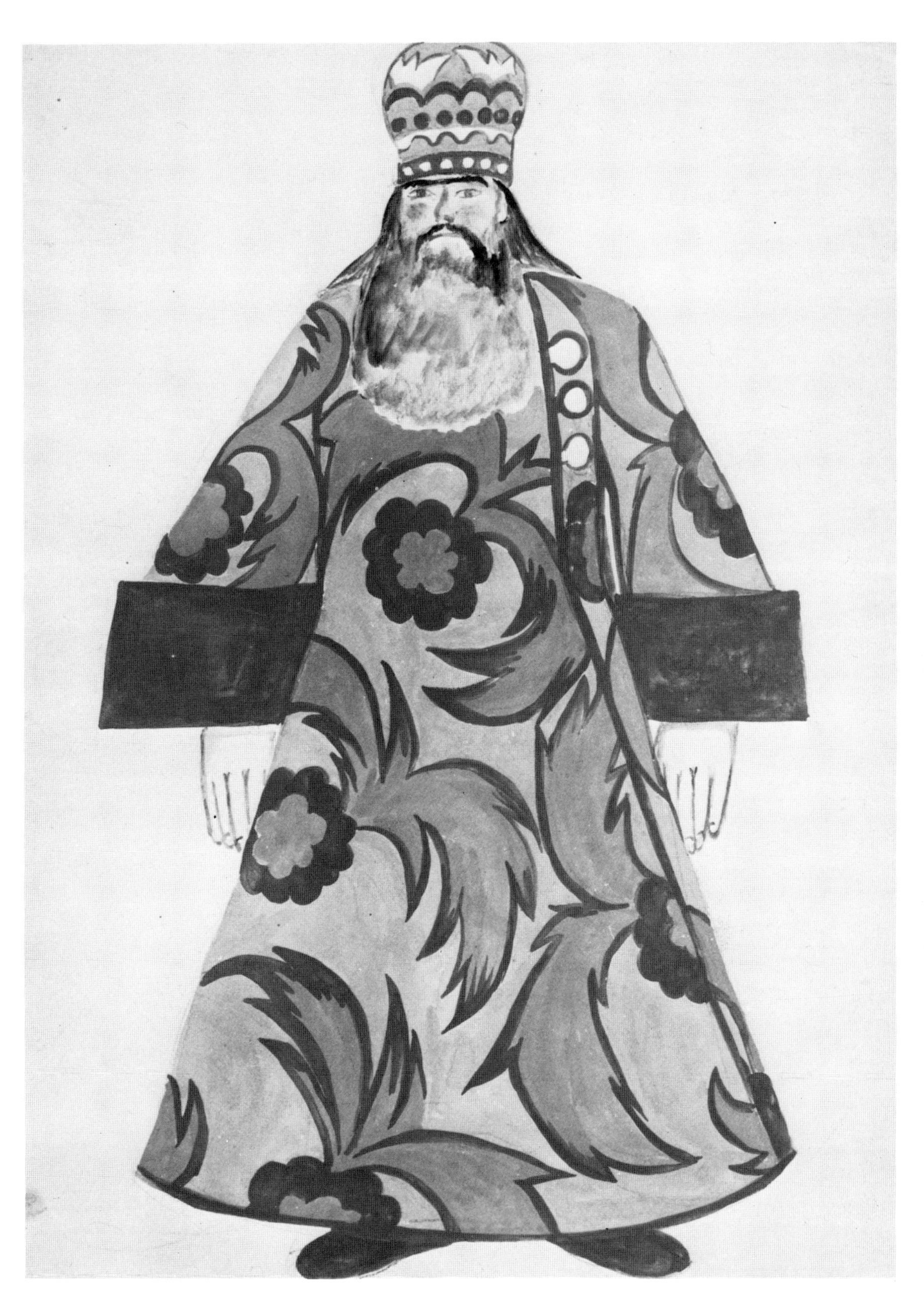

head-dress is shown on the left and the back view of the whole figure on the right. Pencil outlines indicate the sleeveless jacket and the pattern decorating the skirt. In 1925 Goncharova designed the sets and costumes for *L'Amour Sorcier* for Pavlova and her company.

(above)
65 *'Les Noces': A Russian Priest*
PARIS, private collection. c. 1918–22. Gouache 38 × 26·5 cm.

This is possibly a design for the first version of *Les Noces*; the sumptuous vestments recall the style of *Le Coq d'Or.* In the final version of *Les Noces* no priest appeared and Stravinsky explained that the chanting voice was not really that of a priest (Stravinsky and Craft, *Expositions and Developments*, 1962).
1962).

66 *'Les Noces': Design for the Final Scene*
Whereabouts unknown. Watercolour. Signed below left: N. Gontcharova.

In this ballet the stark simplicity of the sets was in harmony with the plain Russian peasant costumes of the dancers. The young couple are seated near the door leading into the bedroom and there is only a tiny window on the wall above.

(opposite)
VIII *Peacocks*
PARIS, private collection, c. 1916–20. Oil on canvas 164 × 115 cm. The signature and date, 1912, on the back were probably added later.

In 1911 Goncharova painted a series of *Pictorial Possibilities on the Subject of the Peacock* and five of these were exhibited at the *The Donkey's Tail* in March 1912, but none of the titles fits the present picture as they were all of single birds. At least five heads can be seen here and both the colour and treatment have more in common with her Spanish subjects and the abstract *Bathers* (Plate 52). The colour scheme of yellow, orange and red also differs from the pictures painted in Russia, where blue tended to prevail except in the designs for *Le Coq d'Or.* The technique includes the use of splashed-on colour, as used by house painters, and the design does suggest sunlight and the Egyptian style more than the Tretyakov *Peacock* (Plate 19). Perhaps it is a later development of an earlier composition.

67 *'Les Noces': Group of Male Dancers*
LONDON, Victoria and Albert Museum. 1923. Pen and ink 44·1 × 34 cm. Signed upper left: N. Gontcharova.

As in the case of the drawing of female dancers (Plate 68), variants and tracings of this group exist.

(opposite)
IX *'L'Oiseau de Feu': Design for the Final Backcloth*
LONDON, Victoria and Albert Museum. (presented by Dr. W. A. Propert). 1926. Gouache, watercolour with gold and silver 61 × 62·2 cm.

The ballet *L'Oiseau de Feu* had been created by Fokine in 1910 as a sample of Russian folklore for the Parisian audience, with music by Stravinsky and décor and costumes by Golovine, whose tangle of detail produced the required atmosphere of enchantment. In 1922 the scenery had been left in a railway siding, while money for the freight was being collected, and was entirely washed away during the night by a heavy downpour. Goncharova designed new scenery and costumes for the revival at the Lyceum Theatre, London, on 25 November 1926. This final transformation scene, when the wicked Koshchei dies and a Christian city replaces his castle, had been omitted in the original production. Goncharova surpassed herself in the beauty of this drop-scene with its enchanting effect of innumerable white churches and golden domes gleaming in the brilliant light against a deep blue sky, in harmony with the triumphant music; a perfect instance of how the décor of an imaginative artist can enhance the dramatic and emotional effect of music and dancing. She had already used the device of piling up churches one above another in her projects for *Liturgie.* Several versions of this drop-scene exist; one, now in the United States of America in the collection of Mr. and Mrs. N. D. Lobanov-Rostovsky, includes the side arches and a garden in front of the churches. Another was reproduced in Richard Buckle's *In Search of Diaghilev* (facing page 97). When the Royal Ballet took *L'Oiseau de Feu* on tour to Russia in 1961 this magnificent finale must have warmed the hearts of many who had never seen Diaghilev's triumphs in the West and Goncharova was delighted to hear of this success in her own country.

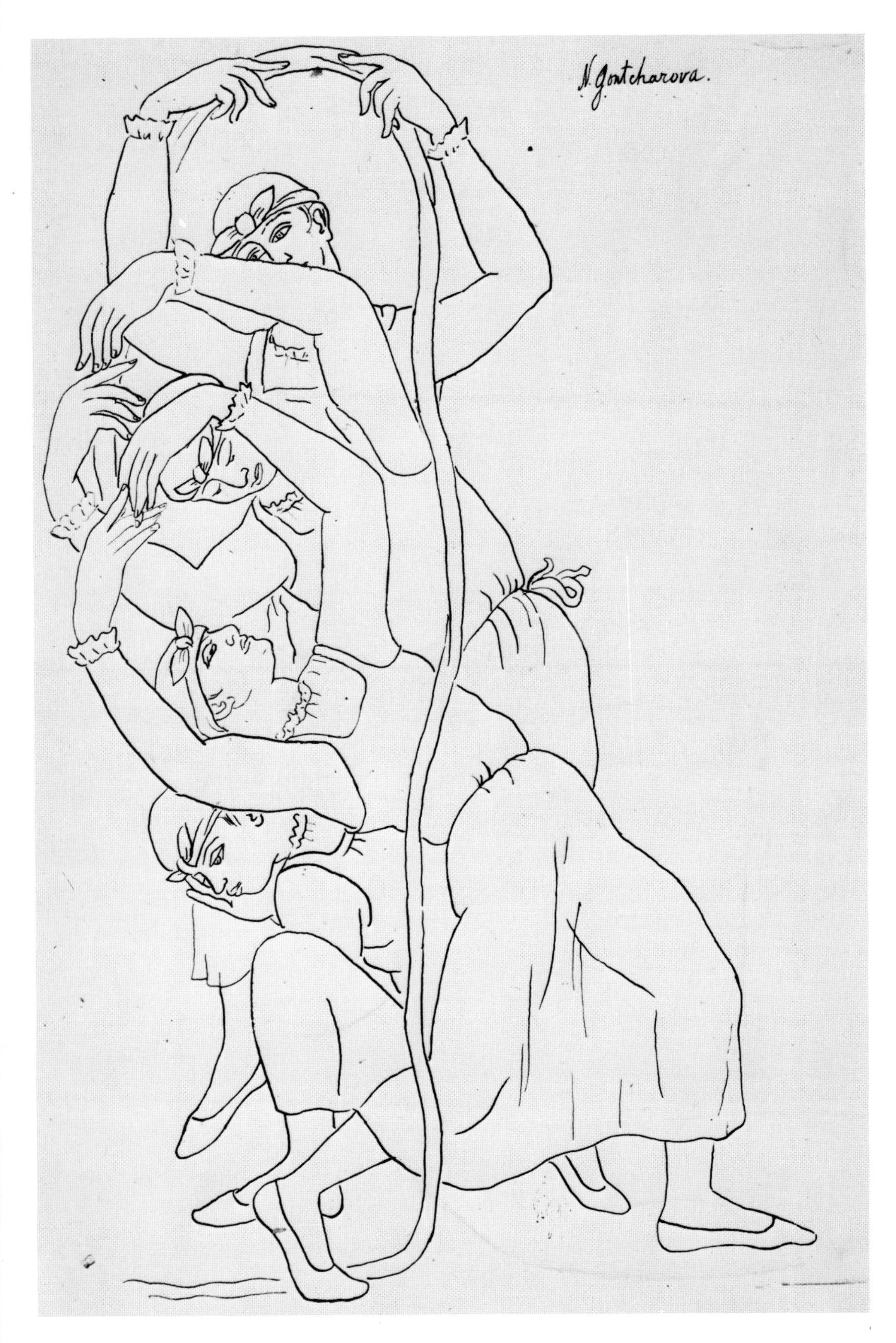

68 *'Les Noces': Group of Female Dancers*
Whereabouts unknown. Pen and ink on paper 40·6 × 26·1 cm. Signed upper right: N. Gontcharova and inscribed upper left: 'Noces' Derniere variante Groupe de femmes.

Like many of Goncharova's drawings for *Les Noces* this is a choreographic study as well as a costume design. Here three girls are passing under the three-metre-long plait of the bride held up by a fourth. A very similar drawing is in the Victoria and Albert Museum, London. Some of these outline drawings appear to be tracings.

69 *'Les Noces': Setting*
HARTFORD, Wadsworth Atheneum (Ellen Gallup Sumner and Mary Catlin Sumner collection).
1923. Pencil, watercolour and gouache 67 × 98·5 cm. Signed lower left: N. Gontcharova 923.

The four pianos required by Stravinsky were to be placed on the stage at the sides. The benches against the wall and the small window and door, indicating the intimacy of a peasant hut, appeared in all the scenes.

70 *'Les Noces': Costume for Two Female Dancers*
HARTFORD, Wadsworth Atheneum. 1923. Indian ink and Chinese white on paper 25 × 27·5 cm. Signed lower left: N. Gontcharova.

As with so many other drawings for this ballet, this one appears to be more a choreographic study of movement than a costume design. A number of similar drawings are in the Victoria and Albert Museum, London.

71 *Head of Christ*
Published in 1920. Lithograph 15 × 12 cm.

The publication of French and English translations of Alexander Blok's poem *The Twelve* in Paris and London in 1920 with Larionov's illustrations has been described by Khardjiev as an important literary and artistic event. Larionov was not satisfied with his treatment of the head of Christ and for the Russian edition published in Paris in June 1920 he asked Goncharova to execute this head and he produced new illustrations. The difference in their styles did not produce a satisfactory harmony.

72 *'Obrazy' ['Images']: Title-page*
Published in 1920. Coloured print 23·5 × 14 cm.

Images was a collection of poems by the Russian poet Mikhail Zetlin, also known as Amari, published by Zerna in Paris in 1920 as a volume together with another of his works *Prozrachnye Teni* [*Transparent Shadows and Images*], in an edition of 1000 numbered copies. The cover, title-page, frontispiece, initials, headings and endpieces, designed by Goncharova, were printed in red and black.

(opposite)
73 *'La Cité': Clockwork*
Published in 1920. Lithograph 23·5 × 13·5 cm. Initialled lower right: N.G.

This lithograph is one of the illustrations to *La Cité* by Alexander Roubakine, privately printed in Paris in 1920 in an edition of 325 copies. The poems are dedicated to the memory of the author's wife, who 'died at her post on 27 January 1918'. The text reproduces the poet's handwriting and the whole appearance of the book, with its heavy script and black illustrations, reflects the mournful theme, in contrast to the lighter mood and gay colour effect of *Images*.

75 *'L'Oiseau de Feu': Costume for the Wizard Koshchei*
SAN ANTONIO (TEXAS), collection of L. B. Tobin. 1925. Pencil on paper mounted on canvas 50 × 64 cm.
Signed at top right: N. Gontcharova; inscribed at bottom left in Russian: Koshchei 1925.

Koshchei the Immortal is a Russian legendary figure personifying death and evil. The name derives from the word for bone and he is often represented as a skeleton. Goncharova gave him long claw-like nails, a spiky crown and drew ribs and leg bones on the tunic he is wearing. A watercolour showing the black and gold of his train is in the collection of Peter Ustinov. In the ballet Koshchei imprisons the Princess Beautiful and her twelve maidens and when their suitors try to release them, the men are turned to stone, while the girls are kept in the castle and only let out at night.

(opposite)
74 *The Swan Princess Rising out of the Sea*
Published in 1922. Hand-coloured print 20 × 15 cm.

The most sumptuous of Goncharova's book illustrations were for the French prose translation by Claude Anet of Pushkin's poem *Tsar Saltan.* The book was printed by Louis Kalder in Paris in 1922 and entirely hand coloured, only the red outlines of the illustrations and border ornaments were printed. Even the endpapers were designed by the artist and there are twelve full-page illustrations. The gay jewel-like colours and lively ornaments are a refinement of her first interpretation of Pushkin's folk tales in the sets for *Le Coq d'Or.* Here the sea is green, the sky blue and the clouds and headgear yellow. It is interesting to compare this romantic treatment with the *Abstract Figure* (Plate 53), in which almost the same figure is treated geometrically, and with Vrubel's painting of the *Swan Princess* (fig. 2).

(above left)
76 *'L'Oiseau de Feu': Costume for a Wife of Koshchei*
PARIS, private collection. 1954. Pen and ink and watercolour 37 × 26 cm. Signed upper left: N. Gontcharova; inscribed below: Femme de Kotchei 12 Costume de soie Cat. No. 197 ; and below the names of the dancers.

In a programme of the first London production of 1926 only six wives are mentioned. In the 1954 revival by the Royal Ballet at Covent Garden the twelve wives appeared, released from their tyrant, each wearing a copy of this dress and standing on either side of the prince and his bride in the final wedding scene.

(above right)
77 *'L'Oiseau de Feu': Costume for a Monster in Koshchei's Suite.*
HARTFORD, Wadsworth Atheneum (Ella Gallup Sumner and Mary Catlin Sumner collection). 1925. Pencil and watercolour 45 × 34·5 cm. Signed lower right: N. Gontcharova; initialled upper left: N.G.; and inscribed upper right: *Oiseau de Feu* personage de la suite de Kachei.

Samples of the material to be used are attached to the drawing. Another slighter drawing of this costume was exhibited at Lyon in 1969 (no. 115) and reproduced in the catalogue.

78 *'L'Oiseau de Feu': Stage Design for Scene 1*
PARIS, collection of Evelyne Cournand.

The ballet opens with a night scene in the enchanted garden where the tree with golden apples grows. Prince Ivan enters the garden and tries to shoot the firebird. He captures her as she flutters about and after a struggle releases her. In gratitude she gives him a magic feather and promises to come to his aid whenever he waves it. The starry sky gives enchantment to the scene and the churches in the wings blend with the final backdrop (Plate IX). When the firebird flies away, the grille (Plate 79) descends to shut off the magic garden and the scene becomes the kingdom of Koshchei the Immortal.

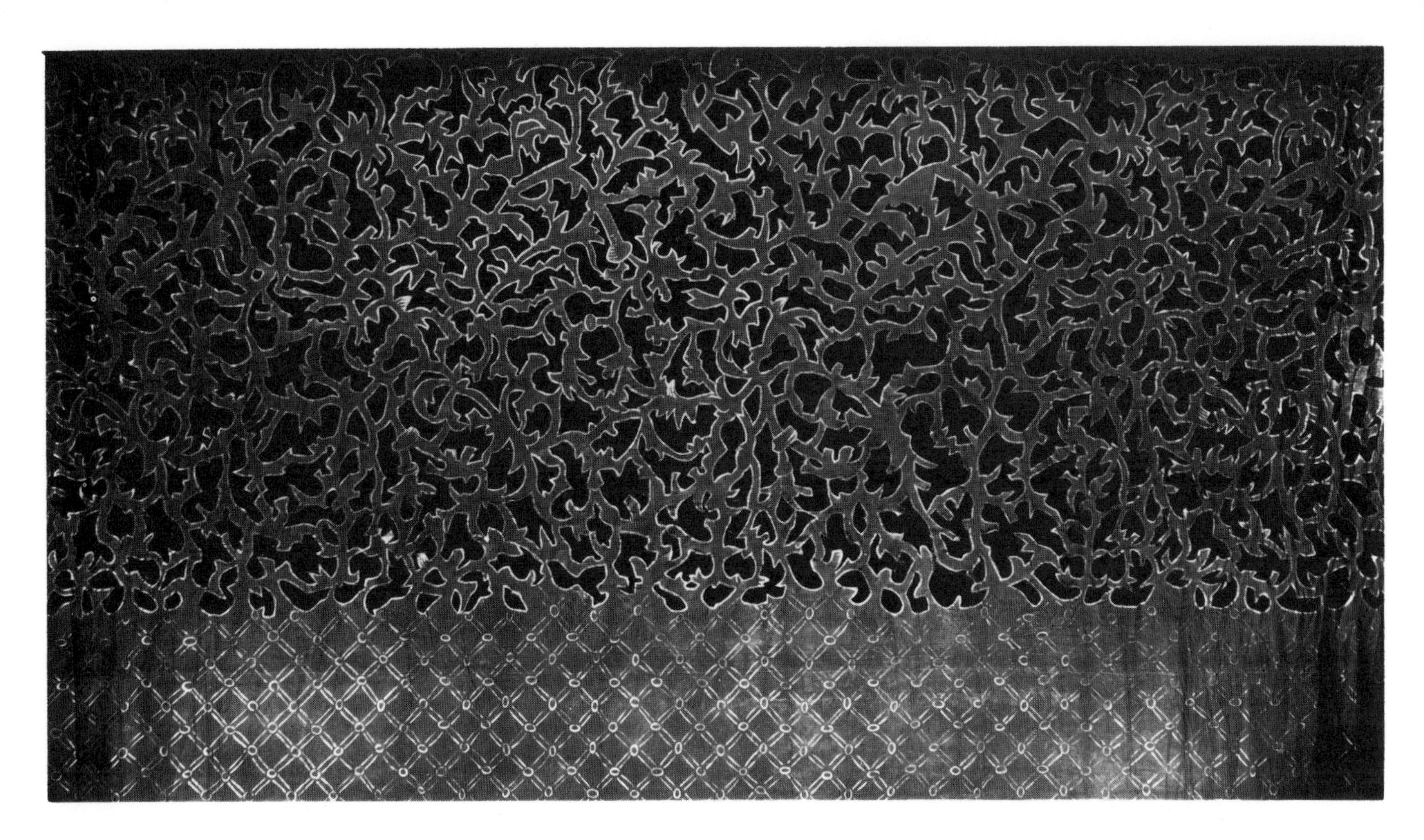

79 *'L'Oiseau de Feu': Stage Design for Scene 1*
PARIS, collection of Evelyne Cournand.

The grille shows the extraordinary care and inventiveness of the artist in every detail of the design.

80 *(opposite)* and 81 *(page 94)*
Russian Warriors Riding into Battle
Published in 1923. Hand-coloured print 26·5 × 18 cm. (each page).

These illustrations appear on pages 20 and 21 of the German translation of the twelfth-century Russian poem about Prince Igor's campaign, *Die Maer von der Heerfahrt Igors*, published by Orchis Verlag, Munich, in 1923 in an edition of 700. The book is printed in heavy Gothic type, with outlined illustrations coloured by hand in ochre, grey, deep purple and black, the colours of *Les Noces* and the Spanish screens. Here Goncharova transported her imagination from the fairy-tale Swan Princess to the grim battles of the early Kievan princes against their eastern invaders. There are several pages of wild beasts and birds in the woods. The decoration combines Rayonist angularity with patterns of crossed swords and flying arrows. The theme of violence is emphasized by the blood-red endpapers.

N. Gontcharova

(above left)
82 *Autumn Evening*
PARIS, private collection. c. 1920–25. Oil on panel 260 × 199 cm. Signed upper right: N. Gontcharova.

The playful improvisation of this angular, almost wooden, treatment of the Spanish theme is typical of Goncharova's work in the 1920s. It is very similar to another group showing two Spanish women with a dog, which was reproduced in the catalogue of her exhibition at the Galerie de l'Institut in 1956, when the artist herself corrected the date from 1915, as printed in the catalogue, to 1922. In 1939 she held an exhibition at the Galerie Cadran entitled *Espagnoles et Magnolias.*

(above right)
83 *Spring*
PARIS, private collection. c. 1930–35. Oil on canvas 183 × 170 cm. Signed at centre bottom: N. Gontcharova.

These four Spanish women in lace mantillas are in complete contrast to the severely stylized ones in *Autumn Evening* (Plate 82). A fairly similar group of half-length Spanish women with flowers was painted for Kussevitsky and is in the New York collection of Mr. and Mrs. Leonard Hutton. Another full-length group is in the Musée d'Art Moderne, Centre Pompidou, Paris. The problem of dating is aggravated by the exhibition of a similar work in Prague in 1935, dated in the catalogue to 1920.

(above left)
84 *'Nuit sur le Mont Chauve': Design*
PARIS, private collection. 1923–24. Gouache 64 × 90 cm. Signed at bottom left: N. Gontcharova.

The ballet was first produced by Diaghilev's Ballets Russes on 23 April 1924 at Monte Carlo, using music by Mussorgsky, with choreography by Bronislava Nijinska. The drawing clearly shows the backcloth as seen through the cut-out arch.

(above right)
85 *'Sur le Boristhene': Costume for Serge Lifar*
PARIS, private collection. 1932. Gouache 51 × 33 cm. Inscribed upper left: 'Sur le Boristhene'/ Costume de Serge S. Lifar; signed below: N. Gontcharova.

This ballet, given at the Paris Opéra in 1932 with music by Prokofiev, décor by Larionov and costumes by Goncharova, was the first production by Lifar after the death of Diaghilev. The suggestion of dancing is particularly well rendered in this drawing and shows the close co-operation between artist and dancer. Lifar was Maître de Ballet at the Paris Opéra until 1959 and did much to raise the standard of both teaching and production.

(opposite top)
86 *'Sorochinsk Fair': Project for a Curtain*
PARIS, private collection. 1940 (or earlier). Gouache 61 × 85 cm. Signed at lower right: N. Gontcharova.

This peaceful rural scene suggests the atmosphere of the opening passage of Gogol's story. The comical cows and angular trees are typical of Goncharova's work in the 1920s. The theme of the girls looking across the water had been used in her design for the marionette theatre of Julie Sazonova at the Vieux Colombier at Christmas in 1924.

(opposite bottom)
87 *'Sorochinsk Fair': Stage Design*
LONDON, Victoria and Albert Museum. 1940. Gouache 65·8 × 81·4 cm. Signed bottom right: N. Gontcharova; inscribed on back: 1940.

The ballet, based on a story by Gogol, was first produced at the Théâtre des Champs Elysées, Paris, in 1926. The music was adapted from Mussorgsky's opera of the same name, the choreography was by Elstor and the designs by Goncharova. It was produced again by Maria Kuznetzova's private opera company in Buenos Aires in 1932 and by the Ballets Russes de Paris at the Salle Pleyel in 1940. The present design and costumes were probably redrawn by the artist from her original version of 1926. Another version of this scene, without the little gardens in front of the huts, was exhibited in Lyon in 1969 as no. 121.

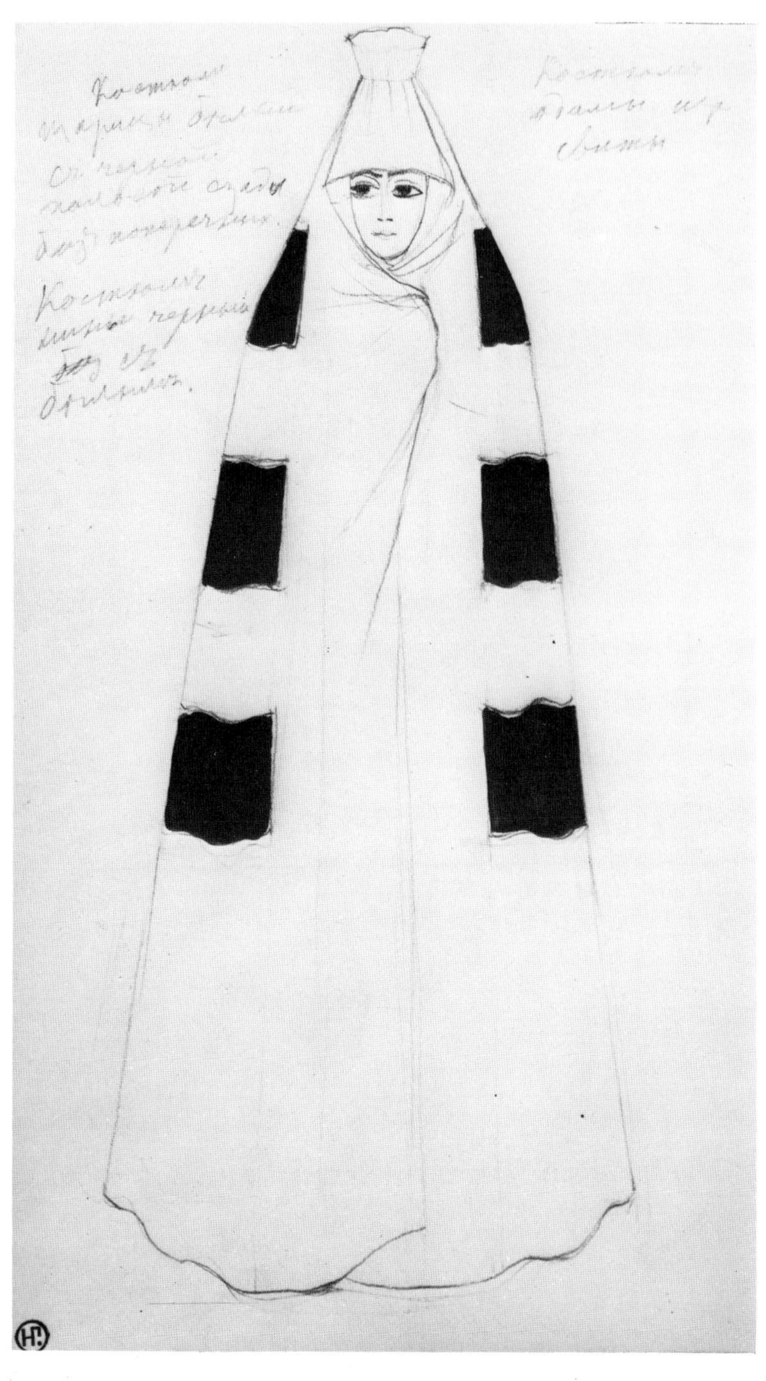

(above left)
88 *'Sorochinsk Fair': Costume for an Old Man with a Pipe*
LONDON, Victoria and Albert Museum. 1940. Gouache and watercolour 47 × 20 cm. Signed bottom right: N. Goncharova.

This gouache is one of twenty-two costume designs for the ballet *Sorochinsk Fair* acquired by the Victoria and Albert Museum from the artist in 1961. The designs are remarkable evocations of her memories of the Ukraine as she knew it in her youth.

(above right)
89 *'Chota Roustaveli': Costume for a Court Lady*
NEW YORK collection of Mr. and Mrs. Leonard Hutton. 1943–44. Pencil, brush and Indian ink 37·5 × 22 cm. Inscribed top right in Russian: Costume for lady of suite; inscribed left in Russian: Costume for Queen white with black stripe behind without transverse stripes. Dress under cloak black with white; studio stamp below left: N.G.

This costume was designed by Goncharova for the ballet *Chota Roustaveli*, planned by Lifar for the Paris Opéra with music by Honegger. Owing to a disagreement, her designs were never used and the ballet was eventually put on in 1946 at Monte Carlo with designs by Prince Chervachidze. The subject was based on the poem *A Hero in a Tiger Skin* by the twelfth-century Georgian poet Rustaveli, who was treasurer to Queen Tamara and who fell in love with her.

90 *'La Veillée': Costume for a Young Novice*
Whereabouts unknown. c. 1940–47. Pencil and watercolour 39·5 × 29 cm. Initialled lower right: N.G.

Goncharova designed the sets and costumes for the ballet *La Veillée*, of which this is one, for Boris Kniasev's tour of South America in 1948–49. The music was by Scriabin, arranged by Nicholas Tcherepnin. The décor included the interior of a church, showing the expulsion from Paradise; this was reproduced in an album to celebrate Kniasev's twenty-fifth anniversary as a dancer.

91 *'Piccoli': Décor*
Whereabouts unknown. Watercolour 32·5 × 44·5 cm. Signed lower right on the door and again below: N. Gontcharova; inscribed on the bricks in the centre: Boris Kniasef.

This ballet, with music by Konstantinov and choreography by Kniasev, was produced at the Théâtre Marigny, Paris, in December 1940 during the German occupation. Yvette Chauviré danced the doll and the quiet sunny interior must have been a welcome sight at the time. The curtain with a pattern of birds and flowers is typical of Goncharova's inventiveness, and the quiet atmosphere of the room recalls the work of her English contemporary, Gwen John.

(opposite)
92 *'Le Marchand de Papillons': Costume for the Butterfly Seller*
Whereabouts unknown. c. 1945–48. Pen and ink and watercolour on tracing paper 35·5 × 25·5 cm. Signed upper right: N. Gontcharova.

The ballet *Marchand de Papillons*, with music by Nicholas Tcherepnin and choreography by Kniasev, was produced for Kniasev's South American tour in 1948–49.

N. Gontcharova.

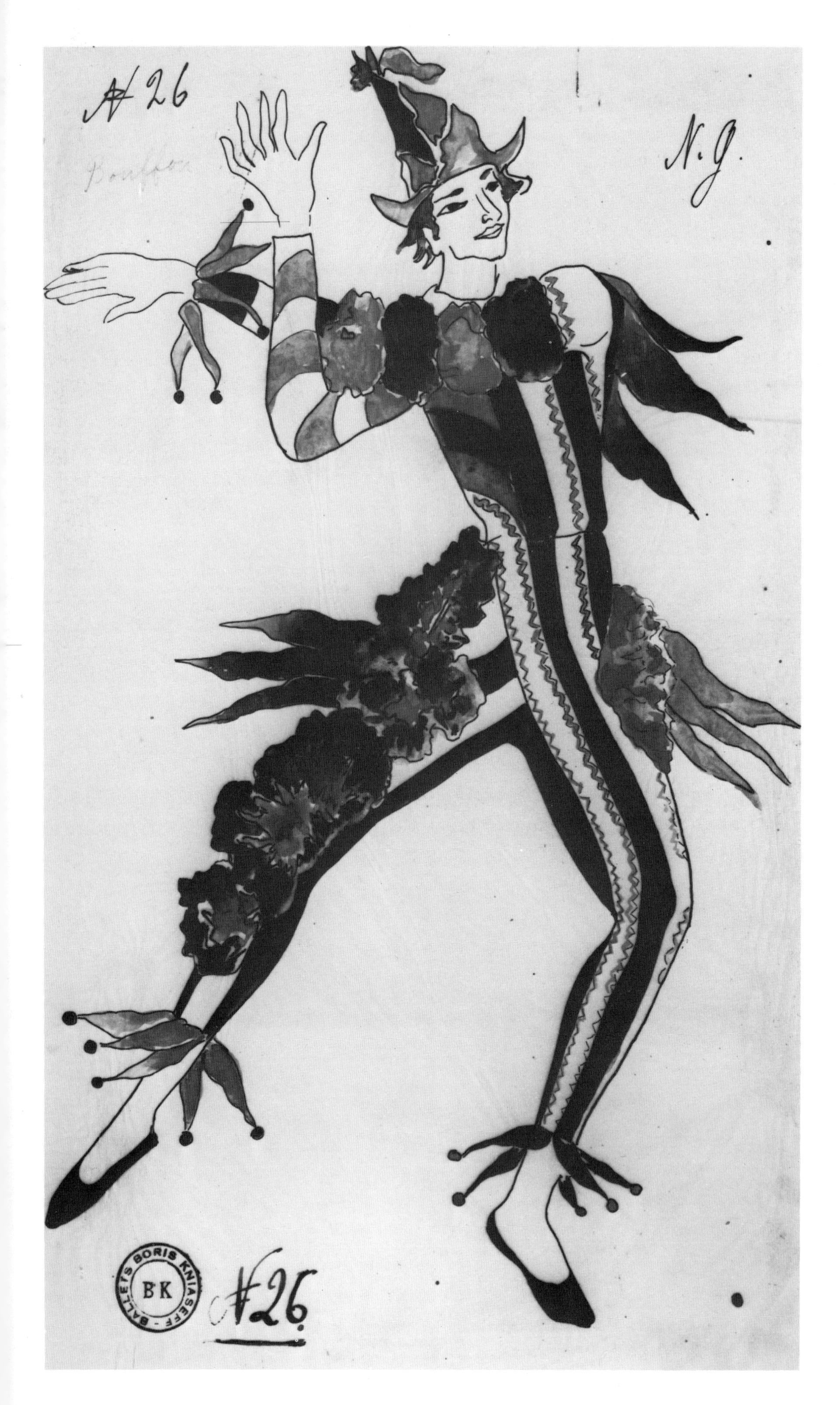
№ 26
N.G.
Bouffon
BALLETS BORIS KNIASEFF
BK
№ 26

94 *'Aux Temps des Tartares': a Tartar Tent*
Whereabouts unknown. c. 1947–48. Watercolour 28 × 40·5 cm. Signed lower right: N. Gontcharova.

This project was for the ballet *Aux Temps des Tartares* with music by Spendiarov and choreography by Boris Kniasev. It was first produced in 1931 at the Théatre de la Gaîté-Lyrique, Paris, and was said to rival the famous Polovetsky dances in the opera *Prince Igor.* It was a great success during Kniasev's tour of South America in 1948–49. The design of rich carpets, hung round a tent, gave the right setting for the exotic dances.

(opposite)
93 *'Le Dernier Romantique': Costume for a Jester*
Whereabouts unknown. c. 1940–47. Pen and watercolour on tracing paper 30·5 × 18·5 cm. Initialled upper right: N.G.; inscribed twice in ink: N. 26; inscribed in pencil: Bouffon; stamped lower left: Ballets Boris Kniaseff.

Goncharova designed the sets as well as the costumes, of which this is one, for the ballet *Le Dernier Romantique*, with music by Schubert arranged by Nicholas Tcherepnin, for Kniasev's tour of South America in 1948–49.

(overleaf)
95 *Space* or *Blue*
PARIS, private collection. c. 1958. Oil on canvas 102 × 60 cm. Initialled lower right: N.G.

Space was one of about twenty compositions on the theme of outer space painted after the first Russian sputnik went up in 1957. 'Real life only began for me two or three years ago, when I began to paint what I will call space. I love all colours, but not one gives me as much joy as sky blue.' These words were recorded by Nathalie Codray-Kodrianskaia, whose *Russian Fairy Tales* Goncharova had illustrated. They were spoken the last time the two met in 1960, when the artist was already seriously ill and lying in bed, surrounded by these latest paintings (T. L., 1971, p. 205).